£8.95

Adventures of an Ancient Warrior

by

Brigadier Kenneth Pearce Smith, O.B.E.

---

*Dedicated to my family and to those
with whom I served in Peace and War*

FIRST PUBLISHED IN GREAT BRITAIN 1984

ISBN No. 0 9509711 0 3

Printed in Great Britain by Stones Printers
High Street, Milford-on-Sea, Hampshire

Foreword

I am not indebted to any kindly person for helping me to record these thirteen episodes, with two exceptions, namely, Commander Rupert Curtis who commanded the craft which landed the Commando Brigade, and to Lt. Col. John Hearn who, whilst serving with 7th Field Regiment R.A. in Normandy, was badly wounded but has been so helpful to me in compiling this book. Thus I have relied on one or two almost illegible diaries and a lapsing memory. I can indeed remember events of childhood, 80 years ago, such as names of the villagers. Yet I cannot remember the names of good friends I had lunch with yesterday or where I have put my glasses I was wearing two minutes ago. Thus there may be many inexactitudes and a few embellishments. Nevertheless, I could testify in a witness box that to the best of my memory it is a true account of an interesting and adventurous life. Admittedly it is somewhat egotistical – I did this, I did that . . . and so on; but it is a personal account of my own experiences and impressions of events with a historical background.

Contents

World War I

In October, 1915 I passed into the Royal Military College, Sandhurst. In view of the casualties in the trenches of Flanders and elsewhere, the normal Sandhurst Course was cut down from two years to nine months and strenuous months they indeed were: 7 a.m. to 8 a.m. gymnasium or riding school, 9 a.m. to 12 noon and 2 p.m. to 5 p.m. a variety of activities, drill, trench digging, bayonet fighting, patrolling, fire control, etc., etc., and evening address by the Company Commander. Saturday was a holiday, but Sunday Church Parade was compulsory. Our instructors were mostly warrant officers and staff sergeants from the Brigade of Guards and consequently the standard of Sandhurst arms drill was renowned. Despite the severity of the work and discipline they were a happy nine months and the feeling of comradeship and morale was tremendous.

I will quote but three of many amusing incidents. One important item in the training of infantrymen is "Fire Control." In this context, on Hartford Bridge Flats, we were sitting down whilst the Staff Sergeant Morris indicated our targets. About three hundred yards below us was a large pool and a young lady was walking past with her dog – hence Staff Sgt. Morris' order, "300 yards, lady passing water, three rounds fire." At that moment our new Company Commander, Major Campbell, who had no sense of humour, arrived and reprimanded Morris and would charge him on the next day. My first Company Commander, Major Hutchinson, was quite a different character and we loved his evening talks. He had served with the 12th Sudanese in Southern Sudan. On one occasion he took a patrol into Bahrl-Gazal where few white men ever came. He came across a village where the tribal chief lived in a large hut surrounded by 365 small huts in each of which he had installed a wife and he visited each of them once a year. I had the temerity to ask the Major, "What about Leap Year?" "Ah," said the Major, "your guess is as good as mine." Towards the end of my Sandhurst days it was announced that His Majesty King George V would visit the R.M.C. on Friday and that a rehearsal parade would be held the next day. Accordingly, we paraded facing the long drive leading up to the College. The Adjutant arrived on his horse and called Regimental Sergeant Major Wombell – a magnificent figure of a man and reputed to have the loudest voice in the army. "Now, Sgt. Major," said the Adjutant, "I want you to represent His Majesty and so get into the car (a large Daimler), go down to the bottom of the drive, turn round and slowly return and on arrival you will acknowledge the Royal Salute." Now His Majesty was a great sailor but he had not a military figure compared with that of R.S.M. Wombell and our merriment was almost uncontrollable. Anyhow, the Daimler arrived, an orderly opened the door and out stepped poor old Wombell, giving the Adjutant a terrific Guard Salute, saying, "His Majesty ready for inspection, sir." Whereupon, the Adjutant said, "Now go back again and come back looking like a King, not a Regimental Sergeant Major." So back he went and on returning quietly stepped out of the Daimler, with slightly stooping shoulders, and was given the Royal Salute. However, His Majesty's Inspection the next day was very successful.

At last the day of our Passing Out Parade had come which was merely a formality. The 300 Cadets of my term, whilst the band played "Old Comrades," marched past the Commandant. Of those 300 I doubt whether 100 were alive two years later. Through the kindness of the Assistant Commandant, my dearest friend, Kenneth Storey and I were gazetted into the same Regiment, The Royal Berkshires, and posted to the Reserve Battalion at Portsmouth. Travelling for the first time in our lives in a first-class carriage, we felt very important. On arriving at the big iron gates of Victoria Barracks, we were for the first time ever, saluted by the sentry which we smartly returned. Then we saw, walking towards us, a martial figure waving a Sam Browne belt and sword. I whispered to Storey, "Here comes the Colonel," whereupon we gave him a terrific Sandhurst Salute which he did not acknowledge. He stood in front of us for what seemed like minutes, just looking at us. At last he said, "Gentlemen, in the Royal Berkshire Regiment, officers do not salute the Regimental Sergeant Major." Remembering how they had pushed us around at Sandhurst, and having great respect for them, we touched our hats and said, "Sorry, sir." Whereupon, with his hands behind his back and shaking his head, he slowly walked away. That day, 19th July, 1916, I was a week short of my 18th birthday and Storey was a few months older, and went out to France on his 19th birthday. He was killed in the battle of Arras. I was told afterwards that he went over the top leading his platoon, calmly smoking a pipe. The next day I had to report to the Commander Officer, Col. Fred Barker, who asked me two questions. "Were you at Eton?" "No, sir," "Do you play cricket?" and I replied "Yes, sir." Although he was my C.O. for many months, that was the only occasion he ever spoke to me. The 3rd Battalion was based on the Militia Battalion (later Special Reserve Battalion). It was officered by County gentlemen of Berkshire – those who were young and fit enough, of course, went to the war. It was now the centre to which all officers and recruits from the various depots, and those who had recovered from their wounds were sent, and I even remember a draft of London policemen arriving. Drafts were sent from Portsmouth to the theatres of war, mostly France. It was sad watching a draft, many of them wearing two or three wound stripes, marching off to the station with the band. Then suddenly, out of the blue, my greatest friend at school, Mat Roberts, arrived. He was older than I was and had stayed at school to pass his "Responsions" for Oxford and we had a happy week or two together until his 19th birthday when out he went to France and was killed on his first day in the trenches. After this tragedy, a subaltern, John Noble, and who was exactly the same age, became my great buddy. Most of my months with the 3rd Battalion were spent at "Fort Nelson" on Portsdown Hill. All troops were sent up there for a short period of battle training and for bombing and mortar bombers, signalling. (I was now a Signal Officer). It was their permanent training camp, until drafted. All Signal Officers from all Regiments located in South Hampshire were sent for a short course at Fort Southwick, where I was privileged to share a room with none other than Lieutenant A. A. Milne of the Warwicks.

The Commanding Officer at Fort Nelson was an ageing retired Cavalry Officer, Major Beresford. One evening he had invited to dinner an important guest. While we were awaiting his arrival, the telephone rang from the Guard Room. At the entrance to the Fort the Sergeant on duty said that a chap calling himself the Lord Mayor of Portsmouth had arrived and, suspecting him, he had put him inside.

An officer was immediately sent down and escorted the Lord Mayor to the Mess. Some years afterwards I met him at his home and he recalled the incident as a great joke.

By this time, John and I had only two more months to go and for some extraordinary reason we were ordered to report to the 9th Royal Berkshire, near Fovant on Salisbury Plain. All 18 year old conscripts were sent here for training until they were aged 19. It was a hutted camp and we duly reported and shortly afterwards went into the Officers' Mess for dinner. Now the C.O. was an elderly retired Colonel who had squint eyes. One never knew whether he was talking to you or to the next man. I was introduced to the Colonel who asked me whether I played bridge. I said, "Yes, sir," and he told me to make a four at his table after dinner. We sat down and the game started. I was just pausing to decide what card I would play when the Colonel roared at my opponent, saying, "It's your lead." He then roared again, "Your lead, Smith . . ." I said that I was sorry but I did not think that he was speaking to me. Apparently I had dropped an awful brick and he sent me to bed. John and I were only a few weeks there: many of the officers were thought to be war shirkers. There was, however, one grand chap, Captain Griffin, who had been in the trenches and who had been badly wounded. He loved to tell them about the horrors of war, at the same time winking at John and me. I gather that after the tragedy of the German offensive in March 1918, the so-called shirkers were all packed off to the front. Fortunately, John and I got our orders to return to Portsmouth.

The War

We duly arrived at Folkestone, parked our kit on one of the two transport ships and were told that they would sail two hours later, so we decided to go and have our last civilised meal at the Grand Hotel. On the way we met two charming young ladies on holiday, whom we invited to lunch. Time passed very quickly, and looking at our watches, we realised that we would have to scurry and we reached the quay to see our transport, with our kit on board, was leaving and therefore scrambled aboard the other transport. At Calais we just managed to retrieve our kit in time to catch the train to Rouen. We reported to the Base Depot, notoriously known as the "Bull Ring," to which all British Regiment drafts went (except the Scottish who had their own Base Depot) and from here officers and other ranks were posted and entrained to their Battalions in the line. To quote Siegfried Sassoon, "I'd live with Scarlet Majors at the Base and speed glum heroes up the line to death." Officers or other ranks paraded separately and marched up to the Bull Ring where we were again given a very unnecessarily tough programme, bayonet, drill, trench digging, etc. by extremely unpleasant W.O.s and N.C.O.s who had probably never been in a trench. The Officers' Mess was an elongated hut with barrack-room tables at which were seated, possibly 100 officers.

The C.O. was another retired Colonel with an unsavoury reputation. On his orders, troops were not allowed to leave camp. Officers were allowed to go into Rouen but had to be back by 8 p.m. – an order which, one evening, John and I disregarded and passing through the green wooden gate, went into Rouen and returned, climbing over the gate which was now bolted, and went back to our quarters. The next morning the C.O. sent for us and accused us of being out of camp after 8 p.m. which we vehemently denied. Whereupon he told us to look at our breeches and explain the blotches of green paint! He, of course, had the top of the gate painted especially and we were forbidden to leave camp. It so happened that the Colonel had a tiny garden near his house and he was especially proud of a large melon he had grown and we saw him showing the large melon to some nurses from the camp hospital. However, next day, we received our posting: John to the 5th Battalion and myself to the 2/4th Battalion and we duly entrained. I noticed that John's kit bag looked remarkably bulky which he duly explained by producing a large melon which we all enjoyed immensely, especially when we visualised the Colonel's reaction when he discovered his loss. John and I now went our different ways: he to Arras and I to Poperinge (where Tubby Clayton started Toc H). The 2/4th had just come from Passchendaele, where they had suffered many casualties. We then entrained for Arras and were accommodated in a tented camp about two miles from the city. It was here that I got my first taste of warfare. I was playing in an inter-company football match and we suddenly heard the ominous sound of an approaching shell and we laid flat. The shell exploded in the centre of the pitch, leaving a large crater, but no one was hit and we carried on with the game. Our Brigade, 184, was in reserve and the other two Brigades were in the line.

However, our turn came and we were in trenches near the River Scarpe. Two companies were in the front line and two in reserve.

British troops going up to the front line and then over the top into battle.

Company H.Q. were 200 yards or so behind and each forward company always had a duty officer in the trenches. As a regular soldier, the day I had so eagerly looked forward to had arrived. I was in the front line. My platoon Sergeant was Sgt Westhall, D.C.M. and Bar – the hero of the Battalion: he knew not the word fear. The Bosche trenches were about 300 yards or so away and the area between our lines was mostly long grass except near the trenches and I expressed my wish to Westhall to go and have a look at the Bosche trenches. He thought it was a splendid idea and suggested that we would pop over and have a look the next day – which we accordingly did. Although we were in the long grass, one or two shots were fired in our direction. Suddenly Westhall saw what he thought might be a sniper's post about 100 yards south and said, "We'll go and have a look at it, sir," which we did. It turned out to be the body of a dead Highland soldier on the brink of a shell hole. I took his identity disc and Westhall searched his haversack and found a new razor which he badly needed. Then looking over the top of the German shell-hole Westhall said, "Look at that, sir, there's a gap in the wire," and before I could tell him that it was too risky, he was on his way, with his rifle slung so that he could use both hands to clear the wire. We were half way through the wire when up got a German sentry (I can see him now, he had a black moustache, like Hitler's) and immediately shot and wounded Westhall who turned round, shouting, "Get back, sir." Then other Germans arrived and started firing and I leapt into a large shell-hole half filled with water. I looked over the top and saw about eight Germans on the parapet. I thought my best plan was to wait until the evening and crawl into the long grass. Incidentally, I had somehow dropped my revolver. The next thing that happened was a shower of hand grenades flew into the air, which fortunately could not make the distance, some forty yards. Then they started firing rifle grenades which were fired from a rifle, rising to about 100 feet or so in the air, then turning and vertically descending to their target. Fortunately, one could see where they were going to fall and the first one was obviously to my left, and the second one to my right – but the third was obviously descending on Lieutenant K. P. Smith. I scrambled out of the shell-hole as the grenade exploded in the water. I then fled into the long grass, with bullets cracking past me and I caught a glimpse of poor old Westhall in a shell-hole and he seemed to be covered with blood. I arrived back in our trench and found the whole line standing to. I met my Company Commander, Captain Field (a Reading solicitor) who, quite rightly, was in a fuming rage and when I told him about Westhall he put me under arrest – and this, I thought, is the end of my army career.

When, suddenly, our new Commanding Officer, Colonel J. H. S. Dimmer, V.C., M.C., of the 60th Rifles, arrived and Field told him that he had put me under arrest, for as Duty Officer in the line I had not informed anyone I had left the trenches and had lost the Battalion's best Sergeant. The Colonel asked me then for my version; on hearing this he released me from arrest and congratulated me on my initiative and fighting spirit. "This is just what I want to see more of in this Battalion." To digress a little, I was understandably disappointed at not being posted to a Regular Battalion but I soon reconciled myself to the fact that the 2/4th was a good Battalion. The officers were mostly business and professional men and other ranks came mostly from Reading, but as Col. Dimmer had inferred, they had had little battle experience and they needed to be shaken up. I took a patrol out to try and find Westhall but the Bosche were very much on the alert and we were unsuccessful. Later I had a short letter from him. The Bosche had come out and collected him and he was in hospital. Later I had another letter from him saying that owing to his wounds he had been repatriated in exchange with German wounded. He said how he had seen me get out of my shell-hole and prayed that I would get away. Eventually, Watney's Brewery gave him a job as a hall porter, and I called to see him once or twice and we had a couple of pints together. He always called me his "Blood Brother." He did not last much longer but he was a grand chap.

A few days after the patrol episode, I heard that another Company was to carry out a raid and, uninvited, I joined them. The bangalore torpedo was exploded to blow a gap through the Bosche wire but the troops still found it difficult to get through, and when they got into the Bosche trenches there was great confusion and, seeing that no one was going up the communication trench, I and another young soldier went up it and were confronted by a huge Saxon soldier. Having my finger on the trigger, I shot him, which I deeply regretted, for he was probably surrendering and the object of the raid was to get identification of the enemy. A few yards further on we came to the entrance of a deep dug-out and could hear Germans down below, but neither of us had a grenade and the return flares recalled us.

A British tank which came to an unexpected half during an attack at Cambrai, the battle I missed!

We remained in the Arras sector for some weeks and Col. Dimmer imbued all ranks with his spirit. In fact, we became known as Col. Dimmer's Battalion. He had withdrawn me from the line and I became his sort of A.D.C. Then, in November, an order came from Corps H.Q. that all certificated signal officers (of which I was one) would attend a refresher course at Pas en Artois. Whilst I was there the famous battle of Cambrai took place and when the Germans counter-attacked, 61st Division was sent as reinforcements and to my disappointment I had missed the battle. The Division was then ordered to relieve French troops in the St. Quentin area.

My Last Battle

In the front line we were thin on the ground. Thick barbed wire fences were in front of the line but there were no trenches and sections dug themselves in posts, sometimes 50 – 100 yards between each of them. One of them in another Company, was raided by the Bosche and all taken prisoners. Meanwhile, fortifications were hurriedly built behind the line – which I will come back to later. On the 8th January, 1918, both Col. Dimmer and I were due for our leave and went home by ship and train together; he going to Birmingham and I to Worcester. Four days later I received a telegram. "I am getting married on 14th, please support me – meet me at hotel," which I accordingly did and we went to the Bride's home and met her and her family. She was a charming young lady and her father was a well-to-do businessman. Naturally, at such short notice only her family and one or two close friends were able to attend the service. The Wedding Breakfast was held at the Railway Hotel and since we numbered thirteen, a bad omen, one old lady insisted that I should sit at a separate table. They had a brief honeymoon. We then met in London and returned to the Battalion.

In recent weeks there had been reports of considerable movements of German troops from the Russian front, now that that country had capitulated and it was obvious that a colossal German offensive, supported by tanks, would take place in the near future. Accordingly, during the next few weeks, all units of the 61st Division, plus an Italian Labour Battalion, were digging trenches, wiring, digging anti-tank gun emplacements and, particularly, on constructing two fortified Redoubts on Manchester Hill and the Enghien Redoubt overlooking St. Quentin (reminiscent of the famous play *"Journey's End"*). Trenches had to be six feet wide to stop tanks, which was absolutely ridiculous and merely presented a better target for the German guns. Periodically, we returned to a hutted camp at Ugny about eight miles from the front line for a day or two of rest and where the band of the Italian Labour Battalion sometimes entertained us with their music and even singing. However, on or about March 12th we returned to Enghien Redoubt. One morning our Brigadier, Hon. W. White, visited us. Recently I had had a reinforcement draft of 19-year-old Yorkshire lads and I posted them to a platoon commanded by an old soldier, Sgt. Dobson. (I was very short of officers). However, when the daily rum ration arrived, Sgt. Dobson discovered that few of them liked rum and on their refusal he poured their ration into his jerry can and swallowed it. And so it was when the Brigadier arrived that Sgt. Dobson was standing above the trench exhorting the lads to dig harder. Then, suddenly, seeing the Brigadier, he saluted him and fell backwards into a five foot trench. The Brigadier was amused, saying, "Poor old Sgt. Dobson," or something like that and passed on. Poor old Dobson was very badly wounded a few days later. On March 19th we returned to Ugny – all of us very tired; March 20th the troops went to the Divisional baths where they changed their underclothing and had shower baths. That night, when I was resting in my hut, an orderly arrived and told me that all Company Commanders had to report to the Colonel immediately. He told us that the German attack would commence at about 4 a.m. A bugler would sound the alarm and the Battalion would fall in and march up to the front. Sure enough, at 4 a.m. the bugler sounded and at the same time a long distance shell landed in our transport lines and did considerable damage. However, we paraded and marched towards the battle. D Company, which I was now commanding, was told to incorporate survivors, e.g. gunners when guns had been captured, etc. We eventually reached a deep and old railway cutting at Marteville. It so happened that it was terribly foggy, which of course was favourable for the Bosche attack, and when we reached Marteville we had no idea as to what was happening in front. D Company was the farthest down the cutting and I suddenly had a suspicion of gas and gave the gas alarm and we put on those ghastly masks. I went up the cutting and, sniffing, eventually decided that the atmosphere was clearer and blew my whistles for "Masks Off." In every salvo of shells, the Bosche included one "phosgene gas shell" which did not explode but, on contact, let out its gas. As I was sniffing a salvo of shells came over and one landed on the bank just behind me,

*A diabolical example of German vandalism in which they destroyed
an exceptionally beautiful chateau.*

without a sound. I sniffed again and, of course, inhaled a dose of phosgene gas. The Commanding Officer then sent for the Company Commanders and he told us that he had sent A Company to establish itself in Massimey and that he was going forward with B and C Companies in an extended line as a reconnaissance in force. "You, Kenneth, are too young to be killed," said he jokingly, "and you will occupy a support position on Windmill Hill for us to fall back on." He mounted his beautiful black charger and went forward between B and C and I took D Company to Windmill Hill where trenches had already been dug. I remember that we were shelled by the enemy and by our own guns but only had one or two casualties.

We remained there all night but not a word from Battalion Headquarters. In the morning, which was already densely foggy, I heard firing on my left and Sergeant Reading's section had shot up a German patrol. On my left flank was a dismounted cavalry division and considerable firing was taking place. I went down the trench to see what was going on and almost ran into the Bosche and returned to my trench and found that the Company had gone! In fact, I was the only front line soldier in the Brigade and despite my gas, I ran down Windmill Hill at Olympic speed and under fire from the Bosche. I arrived at the cutting and found it occupied by a Highland Brigade. I saw the Brigadier, he was on the field telephone to Manchester Hill and the C.O. of the Battalion was saying that the Germans were just coming into the dug-out. The Brigadier then told me the tragic news about Col. Dimmer, who had been killed on his horse. (I heard later that John Noble in the 5th Battalion had been killed in the same battle). My four most beloved friends had all passed on (Col. Dimmer's widow was soon to marry again to an Irish Peer, the Earl of Garragh. She wrote to me and called on my mother at Worcester).

British troops watching the bombardment with H.E. and gas shells of a fortified farm they had just quitted near St. Quentin.

However, I collected a few survivors and walked on and met Col. Wetherall (later a distinguished General) who commanded the Oxford & Bucks. He told me that he had been captured at the Enghien Redoubt but had escaped, and as Brigadier White had been wounded he was now commanding the Brigade, and he told me where I should find my Battalion. On the way, a low flying German aircraft came over and all my survivors fired at it and it came down. "I shot 'im down," claimed one of them and I did not dispute it. I eventually found the Battalion and carried on the retreat and crossing a brook we halted and Major Willink, now commanding, and Captain Darby, his Adjutant, established their H.Q. in a deserted chateau and decided to split the Battalion into two Companies. I was to command the survivors of A and D Companies and Captain Worlock to command B and C, and we were ordered to dig ourselves in this side of the brook, about 200 yards away.

It was a very exposed position and with our entrenching tools could dig only little pot-holes. We were there the whole day – a certain amount of rifle fire from the Germans who were lining the brook, but very little shelling. There was a tremendous battle on the left flank and on my right was a Battalion of the 24th Division which suddenly retreated, leaving my right flank exposed. We retired the next day, being in a bad way; two soldiers helped me along to Vaux where survivors from many regiments were assembled and then to another village some miles away where we met our Quartermaster who, like old times, had come up with the rations and I had my first meal for about four days. However, I was now coughing so badly that Willink and Darby made me go to Field Dressing Station where I was put on a stretcher and ended up in a hospital at Amiens. Before the train started Bosche aircraft came over and bombed Amiens, including the station, which made us somewhat uneasy as we lay there. I landed up in hospital at Rouen and I remember writing to Willink and Darby, saying that I was much better and hoped to be back with the Battalion soon. They did not receive the letter for both had been killed. Both of them good and gracious men.

At last I reached my final destination – Endsleigh Palace Hospital (once a hospital for tropical diseases), in Euston Road, London. My coughing was much better but my eyes were streaming and some abrasions on my skin, particularly my hands. My mother came to see me and was very upset but I made a remarkable recovery, and after a month was sent to an Officers' Convalescent Hospital at Bourne-mouth (now the Town Hall).

I remember seeing on the table of one of the many Boards I attended, the effects of phosgene gas: (1) The larynx; (2) Bronchial tubes; (3) Disorderly action of the heart (D.A.H.); (4) Neurasthenia; (5) Photophobia. Nos. 1 and 2 had cleared up and, I presume, 4 and 5.

I never discovered what photophobia was or that I was neurasthenic but number 3 was the "nigger in the woodpile" and was responsible for my long convalescence – I had sudden palpitations of the heart and one could hear them.

Having received my war gratuity of £250, I led a very gay life. But to my surprise I appeared before a Medical Board who informed me that they were going to invalid me out of the Army, telling me that I would get a wound pension and they thought that it was for my own good. I pleaded with them, as a young Regular Officer it would be the end of another two months. Feeling very depressed, I left the hospital gates and who should I meet but one of my Sandhurst friends, Monty Moore of the Hampshire Regiment who had just gallantly won a V.C. At that time I was allowed neither to smoke or drink alcohol. However, Monty tore off my blue arm-band and, I regret to say, we consumed a considerable quantity of beer and even smoked cigars, and arrived with Monty at Benellen Towers (a subsidiary of the main hospital) much the worse for wear and was severely reprimanded by the Commandant and sent back to the Main Hospital the next day. Anyhow, I feel that my outing with Monty did me a lot of good and in October the Board, to my great joy, categorized me as C.3 (fit for light duties only). I was shortly posted to headquarters of the R.A.F. Cadet Training Brigade near Hastings and caught the Spanish Influenza which swept over most of the world, killing millions. I was sent to Eastbourne Hospital and in a ward of six I watched four of them dying – and was moved to a single room. I returned to Hastings in November and on that great day, 11th November, 1918, I rang up a young lady I knew in London and asked her to get another young lady and book a table for four at Gattes restaurant and, with a friend, Jim Sheridan, duly went up to London. I shall never forget that day. London had gone completely crazy, as happened with the relief of Mafeking in the Boer War. Brass hats were dancing with soldiers and policemen joined in; cabs with people in them waving Union Jacks, etc. etc. After a hilarious dinner we went to a dance and arrived back at Hastings the next day. I then returned to the 3rd Royal Berkshires in Dublin.

Thus endeth my odyssey of World War I from which I returned safe and, moderately, sound but from which one million of our British and Imperial servicemen remained behind. "At the going down of the sun and in the morning we will remember them." I regret that this saga has been somewhat verbose and possibly, in places, slightly irrelevant. However, it was a long, long time ago.

Being back in England I realised how fortunate I had been to survive the most disastrous defeat in our history in which some 300,000 prisoners were taken. It was here that I read Field Marshal Earl Haig's famous appeal to his troops. "With our backs to the wall and believing in the justice of our Cause, each one of us might fight on until the end." Fortunately, the German attack was slowing down, having suffered many casualties and British reinforcements and the Americans were flooding in and the Kaiser's Army failed to reach its objective, the Channel Ports. On leaving the Army, Earl Haig, remembering the thousands of soldiers who had lost their lives under his command, in 1921 formed the Royal British Legion and its motto, "Service Not Self."

Dublin 1918 - 1919

Sinn Fein – Part I: The Lull before the Storm

In December 1918 I was posted to the third Battalion of my Regiment, the Royal Berkshires which had moved from Portsmouth to Dublin. It was the reserve Battalion to which the survivors of the non-Regular Battalion reported for demobilisation. Much to my astonishment, having heard of the tragic events in Ireland since the 1916 rebellion, I found a general "spirit of peace and goodwill," and was to enjoy four happy months.

In July, 1916, whilst our soldiers were being killed on the Somme, a British Battalion was marching to barracks in Dublin when Sinn Feiners, from buildings each side of the road, opened machine-gun and rifle fire and killed or wounded most of the Battalion. This rebellion was eventually dealt with and the leader, De Valera, was imprisoned in England. Armistance Day, 11th November, as in England, was celebrated with joy and relief. One forgets that thousands of soldiers were of the Irish Regiments: the Dublin Fusiliers, the Royal Irish Regiment, the Connaught Rangers, the Leinsters and the Munster Regiments – and the Irish Guards (some of whom were tragically killed in the Falklands). The colours of these old Regiments are laid up in St. George's Chapel, Windsor Castle, with the colour of my own old Regiment. The hospitality, particularly of the protestant community, was truly wonderful – parties and dances galore. I was also invited to one or two R.C. houses. Our Commander Officer was Lt. Col. P. W. North, D.S.O., M.V.O. – of somewhat unusual personality and reputation, on which I could expatiate at length if space allowed (strange to relate, he also wrote his own memoirs, as I am doing, two years later, *"Reminiscences of a Younger Son"*). He was the youngest son of an ancient family with a large estate and mansion in Cumberland.

All seven brothers were soldiers with distinguished service records. He himself fought a very tough war in France, was badly wounded twice and awarded the D.S.O. Unfortunately, he was somewhat autocratic and class conscious and was not very popular with many of his subordinates. Owing to devastating officer war casualties, it had become a very democratic army. But he was very kind to me, especially when he heard that I rode horses and had actually hunted as a boy, whereupon he made me Transport Officer and I had a charger. The Colonel and I, on his chargers, hunted once a week with the Bray or the Fingal Harriers. The Bray territory was in the Wicklow mountains and our chargers could not compete with the banks which represented hedges and on which the horse had to land on and off instead of clearing the whole jump. The C.O. fell once or twice and I fell five times. He then bought two very good horses from the Remount Department sale – a chestnut and a bay. He would send for me to go to his office and his orders were, "Get the trap ready to go to Bray. I will ride the bay and you the chestnut."

Many hundreds of officers were promoted from the ranks – some of them excellent but many others not up to the mark. At that time with all the wartime battalions disbanding the officers flocked to the 3rd Battalion in Dublin to get their disbandment orders, etc. before returning to civvy street; this entailed considerable crowding, two or three to a room. Fortunately, the Officers Mess was very large, particularly the ante-room with a large fireplace at each end and the Colonel and his friends and regular officers foregathered before lunch at the far end and on seeing an officer he didn't know or like the look of, I was ordered to tell him to return to the other end. There were two sittings for all meals, the C.O. always attended the second. When he arrived at the breakfast table every one gulped down their ham and eggs and quitted. One morning, whilst the Colonel was alone and reading his paper, a young subaltern came in and sat down opposite, saying "Good morning, sir," to which there was no response. Somewhat abashed the subaltern repeated his morning greetings whereupon the C.O. called the Mess Corporal, saying, "Corporal, this young officer apparently wishes to talk to someone; sit down and listen to what he has to say." He loved going to parties and had a particularly gracious manner when addressing ladies but he was a confirmed batchelor. On retirement he became a Kings Messenger, spent many years in Japan and was awarded the M.V.O.

I had palled up with an officer named Crossby who told me that a very rich man who lived in a lovely country house near Bray had invited him to a ball and to bring a friend and that he would put us up. It really was a superb ball with very attractive ladies – the old song *"In Dublin's fair city where the girls are so pretty"* proved absolutely true. There was a dance band off an American warship which was in Kingston harbour. After the ball was over, sitting in front of the fire and sipping champagne, our host said that he would repeat the occasion the following month, which he duly did.

However, I began to feel that these halcyon days could not last for ever and seeing a War Office advertisement appealing for officers and other ranks who would volunteer to fight the Bolsheviks in North Russia, I wrote and was accepted. I had some difficulty in persuading a medical board that I was completely cured of my phosgene gassing.

In after years I occasionally met my old C.O., Col. North, at Regimental Dinners in London. On one such occasion, meeting him in the Royal Automobile Club, he told me that he was now living in the Dower House of a large mansion at Box Hill in Surrey and that as he would be away for three days he invited me to stay there whilst he was away. I would find his aged housekeeper, his groom, his horse and, as he had the shooting rights of Box Hill, his gun and cartridges. Being bored with London I gladly accepted this offer. I went for a ride in the morning, shot pheasants in the afternoon and enjoyed his wine in the evening. A truly enjoyable little holiday. But vide my Foreword, my adventures are based upon experiences and impressions, and Col. North is in the latter category. He was a very human but powerful character who had served his country with distinction over many years, both in peace and war.

Dublin 1919 - 1920

Part II: The Revolution

Having recovered from my wounds in Russia about November 1919, I was posted to the 2nd Regular Battalion of my Regiment in Dublin and the same old Portobello Barracks.

Obviously, I had come "out of the frying pan into the fire" and was to experience three or four most unpleasant months. De Valera had escaped from prison and the Sinn Fein had reorganised and re-started their campaign of murders. To quote two incidents: a young officer of an Irish Regiment, who had two bars to his M.C. and whom I met once whilst serving with a White Russian Battalion, returned to Ireland, retired from the Army and became resident Magistrate of an area somewhere near Cork. He was about to attend his first Petty Session, where five Sinn Feiners were to be tried, when he received a message from the Sinn Fein saying that he would attend at his own peril. He ignored this warning, was ambushed and badly wounded. They then buried his body in a manure heap up to his head. He was still alive in the morning and they took him to the sea at low tide and again buried him up to his head and drowned him when the tide turned. He was found later by loyalists. Shortly after I was re-posted to England and "Black Sunday" took place. There was, in Dublin, a large boarding house in which a number of British officers and their families had apartments. One early Sunday morning a gang of armed Sinn Feiners entered the house and burst their way into each of the apartments, approached each officer, some of them in bed, telling them to say farewell to their wives and children, and shot them. That tragedy is certainly authentic – an officer of my Regiment and his family occupied one of the apartments but fortunately they were away. Meanwhile, all over Southern Ireland, protestants were murdered or had their homes burnt – as is happening with the I.R.A. today. This murderous campaign extended to London where the Chief of the General Staff, General Sir Henry Wilson was murdered near his home.

In Dublin a curfew was ordered at sundown and every night British Army patrols, consisting of an officer and about a dozen men, patrolled the city and arrested anyone who had broken curfew. There were comparatively few arrest and our best customers were "ladies of the oldest profession in the world" who, owing to the curfew, were not doing much business. Another of our activities was raiding premises where ammunition was stowed. One night, having just returned from curfew patrol, the Adjutant ordered me to take my platoon to raid a school premises in which Sinn Fein weapons were stored. Accordingly I paraded my men and met the Intelligence Corps N.C.O. responsible for the information and proceeded to the school, posted some men at the back and, with the Intelligence N.C.O. and my platoon, broke into the building. Inside the N.C.O. said, "This is the door, sir," and with my revolver cocked, smashed our way in – and to our amazement discovered that we were in the school indoor miniature rifle range with a dozen or so miniature rifles. Of course, the school authorities were very angry and full compensation for the damage was paid. In this context, of course, it was a war of small arm weapons and incendiarism and not the fiendish scientific weapons which have murdered many hundreds of our soldiers (Ulster Defence Volunteers, policemen and women and children indiscriminately) in Ulster.

Sometimes, when I was not on curfew patrol, I would go out on my own patrol after dinner with a loaded revolver, hoping to catch a Sinn Feiner, but had no success. But one night I ran, instead, into an Irish priest who invited me into his flat. I went in and had a tot of Irish whiskey, but with my right hand near my revolver just in case!

Another evening, before curfew, I met a friend and was talking to him in Grafton Street when I noticed a small man standing by and listening. I proceeded back to barracks and noted that he was following me. I reached the Portobello bridge over a canal and turned right over the canal bank and he was still following me. At that time several officers had been shot, two of my own Regiment were wounded returning from lorry patrol. I accordingly slowed down until he was about 100 yards away and, being a sprinter, caught him up, searched him but he had no weapons, and I asked him why he was following me but, getting no responsible answer, I pushed him into the canal, which was quite shallow and pulled him out. He then confessed that he was obeying orders. I should, of course, have taken him to the barracks for interrogation.

On another occasion I was ordered to escort two suspected murderers to the Assizes at Cavan. With six soldiers and two prisoners, we arrived at Cavan by train. After the prisoners had been convicted, we returned to the station. The train came in and the driver, seeing us on the platform, said that he was not going to drive them to Dublin, which I must admit I found rather perplexing, but an elderly chap came up and told me that he was now the foreman platelayer but used to be an engine driver and "To hell with the Sinn Feiners," he would drive us to Dublin – which he did. I subsequently heard that this gallant chap had been murdered. Later I was ordered to take a very secret and confidential letter to the General Commanding Ulster Command. I was told to take a loaded revolver and under no account to let Sinn Fein get it, which I did without any incident.

Every week I wrote to mother, as I had done in the trenches. I still have the letters which she had treasured, and I likewise wrote to her from Dublin, recounting the episodes you have been reading. But in every letter I received from her she was very concerned at never hearing from me, having read in the paper of the terrible things that were happening in Ireland. Having been posted to the Regimental Depot at Reading before leaving for the Nigerian Regiment, we were very perplexed about this issue. Shortly afterwards, the police raided the Sinn Fein offices in the East End of London. On a table there were bundles of letters with a list of names on their "black list" including my own and my letters to my mother who was then living in West Kensington. It so happened that another house in the same road, the home of a British officer in Ireland, was set on fire. Accordingly, police officers visited my mother, giving her certain instructions: in daylight first look over the veranda and if suspicious, ring the police. At night have a safety chain on the door and a tin of pepper in her other hand, and the police constantly patrolled the road.

After I had left Ireland the Government decided to get tough, first the "Black & Tans" and, subsequently, considerable military reinforcements, including gunners, combed the country. Anyone found with firearms appeared before a "Military Court" and, if convicted, was sent to the Castle and faced a firing squad. There were no Maze prisons! The net result was that Michael Collins, the Sinn Fein Commander, sued for peace and Lloyd George accepted and granted Southern Ireland independence. But De Valera, whose objective was the whole of Ireland including Ulster, did not agree and a battle between the supporters of both parties ensued and they fought each other very ferociously, whilst the British Regiments encamped in Phoenix Park were spectators. In the battle Michael Collins and also Erskine Childers, author of *"The Riddle of the Sands,"* were killed and De Valera won: thus the war in Ulster today.

So I end this summary of my experiences in Ireland, the Emerald Isle – as it was then known. The conflict has been going on for many hundreds of years and will go on until the end of time!

EPISODE 4

Russia

In April 1919, I was serving with the reserve Battalion of my Regiment in Dublin and I thought I had more or less recovered from my dose of phosgene gas which I had inhaled in France in March 1918, but I was still not medically A.1. However, two other subalterns and I were ordered to appear before a Medical Board. My two friends were passed A.1 but the Board (three R.A.M.C. officers) informed me that I was not 100% fit. I was very upset and pleaded with them that if passed A.1 I should be embarking with the 1st Battalion of my Regiment to the Middle East where the dry climate was just what I needed. The Board then had a quiet consultation and decided to pass me A.1. Of course I had told them a "white lie" because, unknown to anyone – even to my Commanding Officer, I had answered an advertisement in the Press from the War Office calling for volunteer ex-service officers and other ranks and Regular serving officers (but not serving O.R.s) to join the North Russian Relief Force. I was accordingly ordered to report to the 45th Battalion of the Royal Fusiliers at Sandling Camp in Kent. On arrival I was given seven days embarkation leave. Meanwhile, volunteers from all over the country flowed in and were organised into companies and platoons and issued with uniforms, arms, etc. The 45th and the other Battalion, the 46th Fusiliers, were undoubtedly the most remarkable brigade that had ever left these shores. The volunteers had served with English, Scottish, Welsh and Irish Regiments, the Guards and an Australian Company who postponed their return to Australia until they had dealt with the Bolsheviks. Several of the other ranks had been officers in the War. One of our corporals had a D.S.O. and M.C.; my platoon orderly had an M.C.

We had, of course, attached units of the M.G. Corp, Field Ambulance, etc. We were issued with an attractive white Polar Star as a Brigade sign on our sleeves and presented with colours by General Lord Rawlinson.

As was to be expected we had one or two in the ranks with criminal records. In my platoon, Private Whitaker was the wag of the platoon. He told me that after doing his seven years as a soldier, he was "behind the bars" several times for hitting policemen, being drunk and disorderly and other charges. He had volunteered for "Russia" as a holiday from prison. My platoon sergeant was Sgt. Sawyer: he had been a sergeant in the War. He was a nice man but not up to his rank. He expressed his wish to speak to me in confidence: he told me of his (serious) matrimonial trouble, and on his return to England he would probably be charged with a serious offence. Could I use any influence I had to help him? I told him that if I could I would.

At last on the 27th, we received our "marching orders." There were many absentees but most of them rejoined us at Tilbury and Newcastle. The 45th embarked on SS *Oporto,* an old P & O liner. The accommodation for officers and troops was excellent as was the food, compared with our daily rations at home. The North Sea was pretty rough but calmed down as we approached Norway and we were ordered to do some weapon training and to fire our rifles and, particularly, the mortars and machine guns. The Australians enjoyed themselves by landing their bombs and bullets near the Norwegian fishing boats. The fishermen were not amused. At last we reached the North Cape and miles and miles of melting ice and the frozen north with a Russian icebreaker in front. It was here for the one and only time in my life I saw that wonderful sight, the Aurora Borealis. We continued through the ice, called in at Murmansk and I remember waking up and finding that we were in the White Sea and reaching Archangel. What a change after such a freezing voyage. It was beautiful, sunny and hot. A tug arrived and preceded us to Archangel.

At this point may I digress and briefly explain why the North Russian expeditionary force had been launched. I merely joined up to fight the Bolsheviks and I think that applied to most of us.

During the World War, when Russia was our ally, as in World War II, we sent convoy after convoy, arms and other war requirements which were stacked for miles on the banks of the Dvina. After the

Russians had capitulated, there was a danger of the Germans acquiring them, and later three garrison battalions, also American units, were sent to guard them. Then on the 11th November 1918 the Germans capitulated and gradually our troops from all theatres of war returned home. But not the poor old battalions in Russia for they were frozen in the for the winter. Hence our title "North Russian Relief Force." But Winston Churchill had other plans. At that time a White Russian Commander, Admiral Koltchak, was leading a force of White Russians and East European Divisions. He was desperately short of armament and other essentials of war and Churchill's idea was to get these to him from Archangel to Kotlas, 250 miles up the Dvina. General Denikin was commanding a White Russian army in the south and the ultimate object was the formation of a North White Russian army to take our place. To quote Winston Churchill's phrase, "I tried to strangle the monster at birth."

However, we disembarked and had received a tremendous welcome. General Ironside, the Commander in Chief, and the dignatories of the Archangel government, our Brigade Commander, Brigadier-General Sadlier-Jackson, received an offering of bread and salt from the Bishop of Archangel, etc. and we marched to our barracks, being jeered at by the American soldiers, whereupon one of our lads retaliated, "The Yanks are coming, say a prayer when we get over there, we're coming over, we're coming over, but we *won't* come over till it's over over there."

We were in Archangel for a few days. The troops went shopping: some of them had been told by their wives or girl-friends to bring back a silver, or possibly a white fox skin. I am told that several Russians killed their cats and profitably sold them to "Thomas Atkins." A White Russian battalion drilled on our parade ground. The Colonel, on his horse, appeared and addressed them. I gathered that he was saying, "Good morning, my children. I hope you are well." Whereupon they answered, "Thank you, our father," or something like that, then they marched slowly round and round the parade ground. Our troops were highly amused. Then were to follow the five most uncomfortable days of our lives. Our whole battalion of 800 officers, plus fourteen days rations, were crammed into a large barge. Of course, we were in the land of the midnight sun and it is at its hottest in June; temperatures were in the eighties and billions of mosquitoes savagely attacked us all. We had breakfast at midnight and as far as I can remember all our meals were cans of bully beef. After breakfast the troops were allowed ashore for an hour or so to stretch their legs. They would play games whilst the tug refuelled with logs and, despite the discomfort of their voyage, the troop's morale was as good as ever, as it was in the waterlogged time of Flanders. It was also interesting to see the Russian villages, of all of which were on cultivated clearings beyond which

Yakolevski, a typical Dvina village, in which my Company were billeted when out of the front line.

were hundreds of miles of forest. Every village had its ornate church with large domes. As I discovered later, the North Russians were devout Christians of the Russian Church. Every house had its icon in its main room but I gather that the Bolsheviks destroyed all the churches.

At last we reached our destination, north of Troitsa, disembarked and settled down in a tented camp and soon settled into a routine of intensive training. Breakfast was at midnight, after which we trained, then dinner at 6 a.m. and training until 10 a.m. then tea or supper. Relaxation until 2 p.m. and "Lights out" at 4 p.m. We all found it very strange at first but it avoided the heat of the day which was over 80 degrees.

On about the second day, two elderly Russians arrived at my tent door, leading a young heifer for sale. I asked them "Skolka roubles?" ("How much?") but they shook their heads and yelled for "Whisky, whisky." As Messing Officer, and having a bottle of that precious liquor, I produced it, whereupon one of them rushed at me seizing the bottle, smashed the top on the tent pole and started pouring its contents down his throat, when the other old boy punched him on the face and started to pour it down his throat; when he recovered from his

A few of the 5,000 prisoners the Brigade had captured during its last battle.

blow the first gave the other chap a blow, and so it went on until the bottle was emptied. Their lips were bleeding profusely and they were completely intoxicated. My orderly escorted them to the camp entrance where they fell down in a drunken stupor. Meanwhile I sent the heifer to the cookhouse where the corporal quickly transformed her into beef – which the troops loved after the infinite cans of bully beef. The next day the two old Russians came and demanded their heifer!

I can remember that whilst we were in this camp there was a freak thunderstorm and a streak of low lightning seemed to hit just some of the tents, causing exposed bare arms to develop a fern-like rash, but which soon disappeared: fortunately, no one was injured.

The 45th was then ordered to the other side of the river, and were billeted in Yakolovski, a small village. Most of the houses were built over the cow sheds where they kept their cows in the winter and were somewhat unhygienic. The windows in the houses were unopenable and we had to smash them to let the air in. We found the peasants very charming and in the village market they all did good business with the troops. I went to the market carrying my Russian phrase-book but every time I tried to buy something all the good women would say was "Niets panamyo" ("I don't understand"). But the troops, most of them remembering their few French words, added "ski," "offski" or "vitch." "Deuxski oeufavitch" in some extraordinary way immediately produced two eggs!

Now we come to a tragic incident. As I said earlier, General Ironside's most important task was to establish a Northern White Russian army and a number of battalions were formed but the problem was lack of officers, who were mostly shopkeepers, small businessmen, who knew no soldiering. By far the best unit was known as Dyers Battalion which was made up of prisoners who had deserted from the Bolsheviks during the winter. They were loaned seven excellent British officers. In due course Dyers Battalion sailed up the Dvina and stopped near our camp for the tug to refuel. Two of the officers, Bland of my own Regiment and Taylor of the Gloucesters, who was at Sandhurst with me, having heard I was there, came to look me up. They told me that they were very impressed with the Russian soldier who was well disciplined, efficient, and terribly keen to exterminate the Bolsheviks. The next day we heard that all Dyers Battalion officers, both British and Russian, had been massacred in their billets. Apparently when the officers were resting, a Russian sergeant and other N.C.O.s paraded the battalion, telling them that their Communist commander was anxious for them to return and would forgive them for deserting, and that they must immediately dispose of all Russian and British officers. This they did, killing the whole lot of them except one, who although riddled with bullets, reached the shore where he was rescued but died four days later. Thirty mutineers were captured and shot: among them was a young Russian woman, dressed in soldier's uniform, who was allowed to go free.

Meanwhile Sadlier-Jackson's Brigade were front-line troops, 46th on the right bank and the 45th on the left. The 45th had two companies in the line and two in reserve, C Company was usually in the forest near an old mill with a large pond full of small fish just the size of sardines. A hand grenade would kill hundreds of them and we ate

The young Russian woman, captured with the Dyers Battalion mutineers, was allowed her freedom.

them, bones and all, like sprats. How they were cooked I can't remember, but they were a delicious fish course to our bully beef supper. Almost every night the Bolsheviks (nights were now getting much darker) would open fire for a minute or two and then scuttle back to their fortified village, Seltso. They hadn't a clue as to where we were and we had no casualties.

We were in the line on 19th July 1919, which marked the official Peace Day (November 11th was only Armistice Day). At home it was a national holiday. Victory parades, etc. were held. Ironically, the Bolsheviks attacked us that night more fiercely than ever. As usual, the Company Commander sent out a fighting patrol to try and catch some of them. Incidentally, by this time the mosquitoes had disappeared but were replaced by a sort of sand-fly, which would cluster around one's eyes, so in the line, patrols were sometimes issued with head mosquito nets and a patrol in the forest would look like a pack of ghosts!

Anyhow, much to our surprise, we were sent up a jar of rum to celebrate the official Peace Day of World War I. The troops soon emptied this jar of rum, the first many of them had had since Flanders. To hear their caustic comments on Peace Day, I leave to your imagination. Private Whitaker's superlative invectives were profound!

We eventually went into reserve. As Bolsheviks had been infiltrating, I was sent with my platoon to establish a check-point on the track, (there were no roads) outside a village. We duly arrived; I posted my sentries and selected a small log hut as my platoon H.Q. To my surprise I saw a bed, and a mattress, and told my batman to lay out my valise thereon. However, the snag was the multitude of cockroaches which in North Russian houses hibernated in the moss which natives put between the logs which constituted the walls. However, my arrival seemed to attract them in their hundreds. Fortunately, I had my tin of Keatings and spraying its contents, I slaughtered hundreds. I then lay down for a short siesta and suddenly heard a woman screaming outside. Sergeant Sawyer then came in to tell me that a young Russian woman was yelling for me to deliver her of a child-to-be. I went out and she rushed at me, screaming, pointing at her very enlarged tummy and then at me. Obviously the event was imminent and she was in great pain and I was, understandably, perplexed. In my three years as a regular officer I could not recollect, either in King's Regulations or Military Law, anything relating to midwifery. However, I had a brain-wave and sent Sergeant Sawyer off to the village to commandeer a drosky – a village cart and the only form of road transport in North Russia, but the most uncomfortable vehicle in the world, as I was to experience when I was carried to hospital on one a few days later. It was made up of long logs bound together and four wheels. The drosky soon arrived and we strapped the poor woman aboard, and remembering that there was a Field Dressing Station a mile up the road, I despatched her there with an escort of a corporal and two men, and I gather that immediately on arrival she lay on the floor and gave birth to a healthy young Russian. Coincidentally, all this took place on the twenty-first anniversary of my own arrival in this world. I can understand the regret of my dear mother and family that I was not at home on this auspicious date, the 26th July. However, the Russian baby would now be 64 years old, if alive.

Next day, my platoon was ordered back to Yakolevski and I was suddenly smitten with some sort of fever and, having a high temperature, my Company Commander sent me to the hospital barge on the river. I had been there a day or two when my batman told me that the Company was going to attack Seltso that night. Whereupon I told my batman to pack my kit and I slipped over to a stranded monitor, H.M.S. *"Monitor"*, who had hit a mine, and asked the officer to put a drop of whisky in my flask as I still had a high temperature, and without telling the medical staff went to rejoin my company.

The Battle

May I digress for a moment. The tragic news had arrived that Admiral Koltchak's large army on its Siberian march had surrendered to the Russians. Therefore there was no point in our remaining in Russia; and moreover, the Trade Unions at home, led by Ernie Bevin, were launching a "Hands Off Russia" campaign. But to withdraw 200 miles down to Dvina would be a hazardous retreat. Sadlier-Jackson's brigade was therefore ordered to destroy the Russian troops opposed to us in their fortified villages and C Company was given the task of attacking Seltso from the rear, which entailed a long march of 7 or 8 miles through the forest. However, the Russian monsoon had started with a vengeance.

I reached the Company who were falling in for the march. Damattos, my company commander, was delighted to see me and Sergeant Sawyer put his arms round me, saying, "Thank God, you've come." We also had a small Russian battalion in our column, and I noted that the dozen or so officers all marching together at the rear, and during the march they would keep on asking me for whisky.

The torrential rain made the going very slow, particularly over the swamps. We were supposed to attack Seltso at 11 a.m. with covering fire from the naval monitors and gun boats, but sadly we arrived an hour later and on emerging from the woods came under devastating small-arms and mortar fire from 2,000 Bolsheviks. Then my Russians, officers and men, immediately bolted into the woods and I went forward to get my orders from Damattos. A Russian battery was blazing away about 100 yards away, and my job would have been to attack them but I suddenly felt as if I had been hit by a sledge-hammer and was sent spinning to the ground. I hobbled back to get the wound dressed when I was hit in my left hand and then in the right hand so I lay down. Somebody yelled, "Mr. Smith has been wounded." I then saw a tall officer walking calmly towards me. Lieut. H. Middleton of the R.A.M.C. knelt down, gave me an anti-tetanus injection and put field dressings on my three wounds. I remember begging him to keep down, for the air was full of bullets, but he stood up, saying, "I hope that I have made you more comfortable." Those were the last words that Lieut. Middleton ever spoke.

Meanwhile, my dear Company Commander, Damattos, had been killed, and the whole idea of a surprise attack having failed, the senior subaltern ordered the Company immediately to retreat. The few stretchers we had were loaded and I was left lying on the ground. Mercifully, my platoon orderly and another man saw me and said, "Don't worry, sir, we'll get you home. We'll go the shortest way – about 2 miles." With my arms round their shoulders, I stumbled along. We met a Bolshevik patrol who fled directly my escort fired at them. I can remember little else until I found myself tied on a terrible drosky and I was in severe pain. At last we arrived at the hospital barge and I was put into a tiny cabin with the bunks almost side by side. In the other bunk lay Lord Settrington, with a ghastly wound in his side. He died that night, and I was taken into the surgery and two Naval surgeons operated on my wounds and extracted a "dum-dum" bullet (which expands when it hits its target and which, incidentally, is contrary to the accepted laws of war. I still have seven little bits of that bullet in my thigh). They also gave me a very effective pain-killer and I remember nothing more of our trip down the Dvina and eventually came to in the Archangel General Hospital, having my wounds tended by a lovely Russian nurse, and then to the hospital ship and eventually landed up at the 3rd London General Hospital for Officers, Wandsworth. After some three or four weeks and minor painful operations, I was able to go out, both hands bandaged up and on crutches.

During their return down the Dvina there was considerable patrol fighting on both banks. On reaching Archangel, I am told there were dozens of Russian officers, which included a few excellent officers of the old Czarist régime, begging to be taken to England, but the two transports were absolutely packed. I am told that all the Russian officers were herded together and machine-gunned to death on a beach.

And so ends my saga, which has of course been based simply on my own experiences and impressions of the Sadlier-Jackson Brigade. I have not mentioned the Royal Naval flotilla which had many casualties in ships and lives or the other forces involved in the campaign.

In the appalling climatic conditions and extremely hazardous circumstances the 45th and 46th Fusiliers did a wonderful job. The Brigade had captured or killed about 6,000 Bolsheviks, probably more. The 45th Battalion had had about 150 officers and men killed, wounded or missing, believed dead. It compared very favourably, in that respect, with the Falklands Campaign in the Southern Hemisphere where, under different climatic conditions, our force of all arms did an equal job of work. But they were professional and we were volunteers. And they received a magnificent and well deserved welcome home and their bereaved families helped considerably. But Sadlier-Jackson's Brigade received no welcome – no help to bereaved families and, ironically, not even a medal. We were told that despite the fact that most of our fighting was after the official declaration of peace we were eligible for the 1914-18 war medals: most of our brigade had already earned them.

In conclusion and looking back on Winston Churchill's declared object "To strangle the monster at birth," it might well have succeeded if only Admiral Koltchak's army had reached Koflas and collected the arms and equipment he so desperately needed; if only Denikin in the south had received more allied support; if only the Mozambique campaign had been successful Bolshevism would have been strangled at birth – and today the world would have been a more peaceful and settled place. But "if only" are unpredictable words. Anyhow, General Sadlier-Jackson's brigade, with great gallantry and many casualties, did their best to make Winston Churchill's dream come true.

Conclusion

An extract from His Majesty King George V's speech, "I wish to express my appreciation of the skill displayed by the commanders and the courage, discipline and endurance of all ranks."

The memorial erected at Troitsa to the 150 officers and O.R.s of the Sadleir-Jackson Brigade who lost their lives in the Dvina Campaign.

Nigeria, 1921 - 1926

Returning from Dublin, I was posted to the Depot at Reading. After a few weeks there I applied to be seconded to the West African Frontier Force and was posted to the 2nd Battalion of the Nigerian Regiment at Lokaja on the river Niger. In those days West Africa was known as "The White Man's Grave." "Debt, Divorce or Drink" were the accredited motives for going there, which was nonsense. Most of us went there for adventure and more pay! In fact the salary of an officer was doubled and white N.C.O.s were granted double service rates towards their pensions.

I received copious letters from the Crown Agents for the Colonies in Downing Street, giving me information about Nigeria. I was warned not to drink alcohol or to drink only in moderation. I was advised to look in a Liverpool Medical Museum in which I could see the liver of a man who had died through drinking gin. I was also warned against the "Old Coaster" who would tell me that, in Nigeria, if you didn't drink gin you wouldn't survive!

Travelling with me to the same destination was Sergeant McKann of my Regiment. I duly arrived at Liverpool Docks and boarded a small Elder Dempster liner, S.S. *"Akabo."* I entered my cabin, unpacked my kit and lay down but on hearing the ship's siren, indicating that we had started, I was leaving my cabin when a middle-aged man was leaving the next door. "Hullo, young man, coming out for your first trip?" "Yes, sir," said I and he seized me by the arm, saying that the ship had started and the bar was now open, and conducted me, unwillingly, to the saloon, sat down and ordered two large Coasters (gin and soda) – for five years I never looked back – but only in moderation! I had occasional bouts of malaria but avoided Black Water Fever which was usually fatal.

Our tours in Nigeria were only for one year at a time and then six months leave, including voyage. For those of us posted to Northern Nigeria we usually took with us crates of whisky and gin and enough tinned vegetables, etc. to last us the tour because except in the larger towns, there were no stores such as the Niger Company, which provided most requirements.

We duly arrived at Lagos and directly the gangway was down we were besieged by a host of native servants, looking for employment. The Crown Agents had warned us about this and to beware of those professing to be devout Christians! And such a one came up to me with his testimonials and wearing Christian symbols, but I noticed that he was wearing war ribands, having been all through the East African campaign as an officer's servant and so I took him on. His name was "Jack." Sgt. McKann and I duly boarded the weekly train up North, changing at Minna junction, and entered another train to its terminal at Baru from which we were to embark in a river boat the next day. It was terribly hot and humid and we decided to bathe and casting off our clothes leapt into the river and were having an enjoyable swim when we saw the natives running down the beach yelling, "Kada, Kada, Kada!" – then I suddenly heard the word "Crocodile" and we swam back to the beach in record time!

We arrived at Lokoja next evening. Hausa soldiers came and collected our baggage and we went to our respective messes. I think that there were about a dozen officers there and they were very friendly to the new arrival. I was allotted half a wooden bungalow and a Hausa orderly. He and Jack unpacked and put up my camp bed. The usual retinue for an officer was an orderly, a houseboy (Jack) and a small boy to run errands and to help the houseboy. My first small boy was named Audu. He was a cheerful little chap but mischievous. One was not allowed to beat one's servants but could send them to the local police officer. I consequently gave Audu a note to the police officer asking him to chastise the boy. Audu then met a friend and asked him to take it to the police with the result that Audu's innocent friend had six of the best.

The heat and humidity was irritating but Lokoja itself was quite a pleasant cantonment and I suppose there must have been about 20 white men, Civil Service, police, doctors, etc. all living in pleasant bungalows but it had a bad reputation for health. One little cul-de-sac

A batchelor officer's normal household staff. My Hausa orderly and wife, my head boy, my groom and his wife and small boy, Auduw.

was named "Black Water Avenue" and another "Mamba Close." The black mamba was a form of cobra which spat between the eyes and temporarily blinded one.

In a week or two I was posted to the Company at Ankpa up the Benui River – a tributary of the Niger and right in the bush. It was a small station, a few white civilians including the District Officer and his middle-aged wife and a police officer with a young wife – and they never spoke to each other. I dined with both families and each confided their opinions in no mean terms. In a few days my Company Commander ordered me to take my platoon and relieve the platoon at Okwoga, a tiny settlement and with no white residents. In this area of Nigeria the inhabitants were very primitive, wore no clothes and the males usually carried bows and arrows, and cannibalism was not unknown. The damp heat was getting me down and I sent a telegram to Col. Hicks, whom I had met on the Akabo, asking to be posted up

North and I received a reply ordering me to report to 1st Battalion at Kaduna.

To digress a little, Nigeria then was divided into two provinces, North and South, each province having its own Governor and separate administration, co-ordinated under the Governor-General and Commander-in-Chief at Lagos – in my time, Sir Hugh Clifford. The majority tribes in the South were Ibos and Yorubas. In the North, with which I was concerned, conditions, climate, religions, character of the people and form of government were very different to those of the South. That great soldier and statesman, Lord Lugard, when he conquered Northern Nigeria in 1904, introduced the form of government known as "Indirect Rule" by the Fillane Emirs of the great cities of Kano, Katsina, Zaria and Maidurguri who governed their own vast areas. The Fillanies originally came from the Middle East and had fairer skins than the Negro and brought with them the Mohammedan religion. The Hausa, strange to relate, are not a race but Hausa is the *lingua franca* of the northern Nigerians embellished by the Fullani Arabic.

The Colour Guard (every one of them a six-footer) on the occasion of the presentation of its Colours to the first Nigerian Regiment by the Governor General, Sir Hugh Clifford. After the presentation they trooped the Colours as the Guards do in London on the Queen's Birthday.

In the North-west of Nigeria existed a large tribe known as Dakakari which the Fullanies had not taken over, but were soon invaded by Lugard's soldiers. Eventually many of them joined the Nigeria Regiment. I had two Dakakari orderlies, one of whom told me the following story. His father had been part of the Chief's household. He, as a small boy, remembered some terrified men running into the Chief telling him that some black soldiers wearing red hats, led by a man with a white face, had fired at them with sticks which made a bang and sent something that had killed some of the Chief's own men. The Chief would not believe it and dealt with them as scaremongers. However, a few days later he was told that a far larger number of black men with red hats, led by men with white faces, had been seen. The Chief went to meet the white chief who was on a horse and Dakakari became incorporated into Northern Nigeria. They called themselves Muslims and, according to my orderly, adultery was a capital offence: the guilty couple being bound together in the market square and a spear pierced them both.

I had now arrived at Kaduna, the seat of the government of Northern Nigeria and the H.Q. of the Nigeria Regiment and of the 1st Battalion. A few of the subalterns lived in mud houses for which we drew £5 a month bush pay. My house was directly opposite the Mess. Apparently, some of the officers knew Jack and warned me to watch my money. I had indeed been missing a few coins quite often. Anyhow, whilst Jack was serving lunch, I slipped over and marked some coins. After lunch I watched Jack go into my house and then to his hut. I rushed out and found my money in Jack's hands. He got six months, I think. I used to see him working on the roads with other prisoners. He was always pleased to see me and no doubt at the end of his sentence he went back to Lagos to meet another employer like me.

Kaduna was a pleasant station and it was here that I became acquainted with polo to which in Nigeria and later in India, I became dedicated. Usually, except on guest nights, we retired to bed early but not so our new Commanding Officer. After dinner he liked to sit up and quaff his whiskies and he expected a subaltern to sit with him – it was usually me because we both loved horses, and I would then escort him to his bungalow. Parade hour was 7 a.m. and the first to appear on the parade ground, spick and span, was the Colonel, and woe betide the subaltern who had sat up with him if he was late on parade.

I had now been given command of the Regimental Signal School to which all four battalions sent their signallers for training and I was promoted as a temporary captain but I had come to the end of my first year and returned home with plenty of money in my pocket and had a good holiday. I returned at the end of my leave on S.S. *"Albinsi"* and had a very happy and somewhat hectic voyage. Some Australian miners from Joss taught me to play baccarat – and I made £36. We arrived at Lagos and Sir Hugh Clifford sent his A.D.C., Eric Dryden on board to invite me to lunch with his Excellency, which I did and sat next to him – but I was not feeling at all well. In the evening I went to catch the weekly boat train where there was always an assembly of friends but I went straight to my apartment on the train and had a terrible night.

In the morning two of my friends looked in to see how I was and were horrified at what they saw and gave me a mirror. My whole face was covered with ghastly spots. Fortunately, on the train was a young Maltese doctor, named Cauchi. He took one look at me and said "Smallpox." The train stopped at Minna junction whilst he telephoned Government House and Senior Medical Authorities and the news was spread all over the country, ordering immediate vaccination for all who had contacted me on the voyage and in Lagos (including his Excellency and the Governor-General). Sir Hugh, I gather, was very angry and had to be forcibly done and had a very swollen arm – and I gather that was why I had not followed Eric Dryden as his A.D.C. It seems that I was the only white man on record to have had smallpox in Nigeria but there was an epidemic of that disease in London when I left.

I duly arrived at Kaduna and the problem was what to do with me. Obviously, I couldn't go to the hospital, so I was put into a dilapidated mud hut and a dirty old man from some native disease camp was sent to look after me. Dr. Cauchi was in attendance and brought me my meals, etc. I was vaccinated and, for the first time in my life, it took and my arm swelled. My face was plastered with filthy grease and, of course, I was not allowed to scratch. Actually, I did have eleven small marks on my face which gradually disappeared over the years. At the end of three weeks or so I was released and given a fortnight's shooting leave at Zunguru and my orderly and a native hunter, Jan Kunni, went away into the bush but found no game and returning to a small hamlet I shot a female wild boar as food for the natives who looked half starved. It was the Ramadan month of the year in which Muslims were forbidden to eat until the evening and even then only frugally, and so the carcass was handed over to the villagers and I was carved a chop. I told my orderly and Jan Kunni, who professed to be devout Mohammedans that, of course, it was only midday and moreover Mohammed had ordained that as a wild pig has shown him the way to a well in the desert when he was dying of thirst none of his followers should ever eat the flesh of a pig. The poor old chaps looked very sad for they were very hungry and in a few minutes came to me, saying that Mohammed had said that under great privation the Prophet had ordained that they could eat a little and I agreed that this was such an occasion and they went and had a good meal of wild pork. Later on they came to me, begging me not to tell anybody in the battalion of how they had transgressed!

A few weeks later I was invalided home on S.S. *"Abinsi"* where I did not get a popular reception – as the person responsible for them being forcibly vaccinated, especially the Captain who, with a swollen arm, was not his usual kind self.

In six months I returned to Nigeria for my last tour and reported at Kaduna and the Signal School, first at Zaria and then at Kano. I had now got a good headboy and a new small boy, named Sambo. In the cold weather, and it can be very cold with winds from the Sahara desert, I would have some hot water in my evening tub and Sambo's job was to fill the tub and stand by with my towel. Sambo was absolutely coal black with enormous eyes and watching me bathe he would lick his lips with his tongue. I asked every night why he was doing this and he said he was thinking how nice I would taste. His story was that when he was a tiny boy his father came back with a dead white man and gave him a bit to taste and it was delicious. Apparently, his tribe were cannibals and soldiers were sent to destroy the village and the villagers all fled into the bush, leaving poor little Sambo behind and the soldiers brought him back and looked after him.

At Kaduna, Zaria and Kano I played polo and also bought and trained ponies for racing, which was very much in my family blood. Race meetings were great occasions. One could buy a good race pony for a tenner and I won many races, especially with "Maiwand" which I eventually I sold to a Lagos businessman for £132. He twice won the Governor's Cup – the Nigerian Derby. A word about the Hausa

My racing pony, Maiwand.

soldiers of whom I became very fond and I learned their language fluently. They had a good fighting record in the East African Campaign (World War I) and in Burma in World War II. They were loyal, disciplined and had a great sense of humour. My signallers loved signalling especially when sending rude messages to their friends by heliograph from their distant locations. One day, two ladies, a rarity in Northern Nigeria in those days, suggested that the soldiers might appreciate a competition for the best kept hut and most attractive wife. The soldiers lived in small round huts with their (so-called) wives which few of them were. They thought it a wonderful idea and spent hours decorating their huts and the women their costumes. My sergeant and his genuine wife, who was somewhat corpulent, were particularly resplendent both in costume and hut decoration. However, there was one particularly attractive and fair-skinned Fullani girl and her hut was accorded the prize. The next morning the sergeant was very morose and obviously upset and I asked him why. He said that the ladies had made a wrong decision for everyone agreed that his wife and their hut was the obvious winners.

The Signal School at Kano during a course. Note the heliographs.

And now for my last episode. The Hausa inhabitants of Northern Nigeria were exceedingly loyal to the King of Great Britain. All government and military buildings, equipment, etc. belonged to the "Sariki" (King) and all officers and government officials were representatives of the Sariki and they would bow and call one "Zaki" (Lion) when one passed by. One can imagine the excitement when they heard the eldest son of His Majesty the King ("Dan Sariki") was about to visit Kano.

In 1929 H.R.H. the Prince of Wales was on a tour of the British Empire in a battleship. He arrived at Lagos and was received with great ceremony and festivities. The next day H.R.H. and Sir Hugh Clifford started their journey to Kano. For part of the journey the Prince of Wales insisted on driving the engine. Arriving at Kano he was received by and inspected a Royal Guard of Honour of the 2nd Nigeria Regiment and driven to the Resident's house. Several troops had been brought to Kano from outstations for the occasion and officers were sitting in a circle outside the officers mess when, out of the evening mist, appeared a slight figure wearing shorts and a vest and carrying a tennis racquet. Recognising H.R.H., as Kano garrison C.O., I went to meet him and he asked if he might sit down and have a chat with us. He sat down and asked many questions about our lives in Nigeria, sitting next to me. I remember him saying that of all the Royal Family he paid greatest tribute to his brother's wife (now H.M. the Queen Mother). Getting up, he said how very interested and delighted he was to have met us.

I had been told to arrange a polo match for the next day – a Kano team versus the Governor-General's team, including H.R.H. In the game my job was to mark H.R.H. In the third chukka he got away with the ball and whilst the spectators cheered he raced towards the goal, whilst I rode beside him, wanting him to score, when he yelled at me asking why in blazes I did not ride into him – which I did, nearly knocking him off his saddle. He recovered and yelled at me, "That's better."

The next day there took place the most impressive and spectacular Durbar that ever was – or will be. Thousands of tribal chiefs, great and small, and their warriors all mounted, from all parts of Northern Nigeria, rode past His Royal Highness, shouting and raising their spears in salute. Some of the Fullanis, I believe, were wearing weapons captured in the crusades of Richard Coeur de Lion's period!

The visit of H.R.H. The Prince of Wales to Kano. This photograph was taken between chukkas. On the left, the umpire, the Prince's valet, Col. Badham, the Commandant, H.R.H. and the author.

That evening a farewell ball was arranged; a dance floor had been erected over a dry pool, just how I cannot remember. We all filed past the Prince and introduced ourselves. In front of me was an employee of the Niger Company. The Prince, looking at him, said, "We have met before, at the battle of Cambrai in 1917. We were walking up the road which the Bosche started to shell and we leapt into a ditch until the shelling stopped." "Quite right, sir," said the man.

Then came the ball. A very pretty young lady, a rarity in Nigeria in those days, and I booked the first and other dances. We were dancing when H.R.H.'s eyes and those of the young lady met – and I said to her, "I think this is our first and last dance." Sure enough, an equerry approached her and said that H.R.H. would like to meet her and, sure enough, it was our first and last dance! Whether he would have made a good King, as a member of the public, it's not for me to surmise, but he was a very human and attractive personality.

Amongst the many interesting people I met in Nigeria was a well known missionary, the Rev. Bargery. He had translated some of the Old Testament into Hausa which helped me considerably when studying for my Higher Standard Examination. One of his stories was when boating up the river Niger he saw a huge crocodile on the beach with dozens of natives hanging on to its tail whilst others were spearing it. As he landed they were cutting the animal open and to his horror he saw a dead white baby. He then realised that it was the body of an albino baby, which had obviously been thrown into the river, dead or alive.

On another occasion, at one of the villages on the Niger where there was a missionary school, as the Niger was infested with crocodiles a crocodile proof swimming pool had been constructed. An opening ceremony was accordingly arranged in which the head-boy was to dive off the board into the pool. Many spectators, white and black, attended and applauded as the boy dived into the pool but never to reappear. A large crocodile had been either enclosed during the construction or somehow had burrowed in beneath.

Pegleg Walker had for many years run a little trading station on the banks of the Niger. On the outbreak of the South African war he volunteered to fight the Boers and lost a leg – hence his name. Returning, he married a native woman who proceeded to produce a child every year, mostly boys, I think. Whilst aboard a two-cabin craft which carried passengers and cargo we stopped for a while at Pegleg station. To my amazement, on the bank was Pegleg, his wife and about twelve children, all standing in line, tallest on the right and shortest on the left, in true military style. He then ordered "Left turn. Right wheel," and across the gangway into the boat. As I had to disembark shortly afterwards I did not get a chance to meet him.

I was then sent down to Zaria to command the Regimental Depot, Signallers and a Mountain battery. But my time had come to quit. Passing through Kaduna, as the train started, the buglers of the 1st Battalion on the platform blew "The Hausa Farewell," which was customary when an officer left for home after his last tour. I felt very emotional for I loved my Hausa soldiers. Thus ended five of the happiest years of my long life.

A Gold Coast Interlude

The Inspector-General of the West African Frontier Force ordained that all officers, especially of the Gold Coast (Ghana) and Nigerian Regiments, should pass an elementary test in Hausa – otherwise they would not return for another tour.

Being almost bilingual in Hausa I was therefore ordered to visit the Gold Coast (Ghana) and all officers of the infantry and gunners would be tested. Reaching Accra I disembarked into a boat and rowed ashore, in those days the only means of getting ashore. Arriving, I was surprised to see a bunch of officers who ran down to meet me and help with my baggage. They took me up to the Mess where they were very hospitable and arranged a game of polo the next day: they couldn't have been kinder and, of course, I knew the reason for this excessive bonhomie. However, in the next day or two, I tested them all individually, asking them simple questions, e.g. "If you were very thirsty and wanted a drink, how would you ask for it in Hausa?" I simply had to fail three officers but they still had six months to go before their tour ended. I then went up to Kumassi, right up in the North, bordering on the Sahara. It had once been a separate kingdom. There were two infantry companies there and, I think, some gunners. Captain Valentine of the Devons (who many years later was one of my C.O.s in my Malta Brigade was their Commander). They had a tremendous party to welcome me which continued for many hours.

(My son, who was in Ghana on a civilian job some thirty years later, visited the mess and saw his old Dad's signature in the guest book). I found that most of the officers in Kumassi had a smattering of Hausa and I passed all of them. I asked if I might see their soldiers who were paraded and told them to sit down whilst I gave them a talk in Hausa, which delighted them.

I returned to Accra to catch my boat but not before the three officers whom I had failed took me to dinner to show that there was no ill feeling. Again a happy fortnight – and look at poor old Ghana now!

The General Strike, 1926

I had finished my tour of service in Nigeria and was on leave pending posting. The silence in the London streets was somewhat eerie – no buses, trains or taxis, and no newspapers. I joined a long queue at Scotland Yard, in Whitehall, of volunteers eager to be given a task. When asked what tasks I wished to undertake, I said "A Special Constable," and was posted to Rochester Row Police Station and reported to the Chief Inspector – a terrific chap both in stature and personality. Hearing that I was an army officer, he ordered me to take a squad of volunteers and to post them at the entrances of Battersea Power Station. I was issued with a truncheon, a police whistle and a plate number "42". We were to hide our truncheons and keep together but not to look like policemen. As we went along as a group the people on the pavements wondered who we were – some thought we were strike pickets and so we seemed to be popular. I posted my troop for their six-hour duty.

My next job, with two or three others, was to accompany the Inspectors to a strike meeting nearby. A small platform had been erected and strike leader was about to address the assembly when we arrived. The Inspector stood beside the speaker and told him to carry on. The speaker started, "Comrades . . ." whereupon the Inspector roared at him, "I don't want to hear any of that nonsense" – which unnerved the speaker and the assembled meeting gradually broke up.

Another evening I was told to take a few of my other Specials to Battersea bridge. The pubs on the Battersea side closed at 10 p.m. whilst on the Rochester side, they closed at 10.30 p.m. and, although this was a normal occurence, the Inspector thought the police would appreciate our support at the somewhat explosive time. However, it all went off peacefully for us custodians of the law and the beer-drinkers were able to enjoy their pints on both sides of the bridge.

Next day I happened to be at the police station when the Inspector, who had just been on the phone, turned to me and told me to hurry down the Thames Embankment to the Lambeth crossroads where traffic conditions were chaotic. I arrived there in a few minutes and indeed the traffic situation was chaotic but I did not see what I could do to solve it. As I stood contemplating the chaos, an angry person seeing that I was a Special Constable, rushed up, telling me that a Special Constable should be taking action and not just standing and looking. Whereupon I blew my whistle, raised my truncheon and walked into the middle of the congestion. It was not an act of gallantry because none of the traffic was moving and despite my efforts the crisis was not solved: in fact, it deteriorated. Suddenly I was seized by the collar by a huge policeman who pushed me aside and with his whistle and his truncheon, got the traffic moving again!

By now, about the fifth day of the strike, Special Constable Police Posts had been established at the most important places in a divisional area, from Battersea to Marble Arch. It was my job to visit these posts once a day. It so happened that one of these posts was the Crown Agents for the Colonies in Downing Street, just opposite No. 10. For these visits, I was allocated for the first time in my life, a cheauffeur-driven Rolls Royce (loaned, of course, to the police). I duly arrived in Downing Street and to my dismay could find no Special Constables. I asked a policeman outside No. 10 and he told me that there had been four gentlemen there but they had gone into the next house, No. 11. I went to No. 11, rang the bell fiercely and the butler arrived and told me that four gentlemen had arrived for tea and he would report my arrival. He returned and led me to a room in which my four "deserters" and others were having tea. I told them to return to their posts immediately – telling me that I was quite right, they gulped down their tea, and apologising to their hosts, we quitted No. 11. I did not know that I had virtually forced an entrance into the house of the Chancellor of the Exchequer and had interrupted his tea-party.

The next day, the General Strike of 1926 had ended. Of course, the main object of my writing this volume has been to record my career. However, I have included this short episode because it was an historical event. The response to the call for volunteers to take on all sorts of jobs exceeded all expectations. It was indeed a resurgence of patriotism. Anyhow, I am glad of my infinitesimal part and still treasure my truncheon, my whistle and my number "42".

W E DESIRE on behalf of His Majesty's Government to thank you in common with all others who came forward so readily during the crisis and gave their services to the Country in the capacity of Special Constables.

Stanley Baldwin

PRIME MINISTER.

W Joynson Hicks

HOME SECRETARY.

Downing Street,
May, 1926.

To *K. P. Smith Esq.*

METROPOLITAN SPECIAL CONSTABULARY RESERVE.

The message sent by the Government to those who served as Special Constables.

India

On returning from Nigeria in 1926, I was posted to the second Battalion (the 66th) of my Regiment, stationed as a unit of the Army of Occupation, at Bingen and Wiesbaden. Under the Cardwell System, every Infantry Regiment (with exceptions) consisted of two battalions, one of which was kept at full strength abroad. The home battalion, with regular officers and N.C.O.s, were about half strength and sent the drafts to the overseas battalion. On the outbreak of war the battalion was brought up to strength with reservists and took part in the tragic retreat from Mons. The first Battalion (the 49th) came from India and in their first battle at Ypres were decimated.

Thus there was great enmity between the first (49th) and second (66th) Battalions (as happened in many regiments), the latter regarding newcomers from overseas as foreigners, as I apparently was. One day I received a letter from a wealthy officer in the Regiment saying that he had been posted to India and he offered me £300 to go in his place, which I indignantly refused; another officer avidly accepted the offer and off he went. Ironically, a day or two later, I received a letter from the War Office posting me to India. On my way back I decided to spend a few days at La Zoute and Knocke in Belgium and in the bar of the hotel I met the C.I.G.S. General, the Earl of Cavan. I told him my story. He was very sympathetic and told me to see him in the War Office which I did not do for my heart was really set on going to India, but the fact that the 66th officers always stayed at home annoyed me. Actually, with one or two exceptions, they were a very friendly bunch and played their part in World War II – but that £300 would have been very, very acceptable!

Otherwise my year at Wiesbaden was not particularly eventful. I went to France for two months to study for my interpretership.

I played my last game of rugger in the final of the Rhine Army Cup, was counted out and received a "Good Loser" medal in the Rhine Army Boxing championship and watched the wonderful Pavlova in her "Dying Swan."

My next seven years were to be spent in India – then "the brightest jewel in the British Crown." I travelled aboard a trooper and after a very cheerful voyage, in which I met several friends, I landed at Bombay and proceeded to Fyzabad, a delightful station on the banks of the Gogra which is a tributary of the River Ganges. I initiated polo and some subalterns became very keen, and I myself was initiated into "pig sticking," a very perilous sport, both for the rider, the horse and the boar. A Rajput Battalion and a Gunner Battery (Tombs Troop) were likewise stationed there and became great polo friends. The Brigade H.Q. was at Lucknow about 60 miles away, the siting of the historic siege in the Indian Mutiny.

Sadly, after a year, we were moved to Dinapur in Bihar, near Patna and about 50 miles from Calcutta. It was a most dismal station with barracks built long before the Mutiny. A few miles away was the village of Budgaya, so named because it was here that Buddha took his first step in his attempt to cross the world in seven steps and there was the imprint of an enormous foot.

For the next six months "C" company was sent to our outpost station at Muzaffapur, a delightful spot with new barracks, a few married quarters and a large *maidan* (open space), including a polo ground. Unfortunately, it was the period of the Gandhi riots and the soldiers were confined to that area.

Now a word about the British soldiers in India, most of them having to spend five years in India. During my five years, I commanded "C" company and we got to know one another very well. A draft from the U.K. arrived every year, many of them of poor physique and looking half-starved, but at the end of their five years they went home fine, upstanding men. "C" company won every Battalion trophy including the light-heavyweight boxing belt of India, by Private Pockett. I was always very keen on boxing and one day Pockett came to the orderly room and said he was going to give it up. I asked him why and he said that no one was prepared to spar (train) with him. "All right, Pockett," I said, "meet me in the gym at 7 p.m. and promise not to hit me too hard," which he promised. At the appointed hour we started and within seconds I was on the receiving end of one or two mighty blows. I yelled at him: "All right, sir," said he and I received another straight left in the face. I happened to look up a the gym windows which were full of faces which disappeared when they saw me looking – and for the next few days I had "two beautiful black eyes."

There was another remarkable character named Private Walters. In World War I he was a stretcher-bearer and on many occasions attended or collected the wounded in No Man's Land under intense fire and was awarded the D.C.M. and bar. He had been educated at a minor Public School but his trouble was "the bottle." I made him responsible for the education of twenty or so children of my married families. One day he was seen leading the children along the balustrade at the top of the barracks, with the terrified parents watching from below. During the years he had several times been promoted to Sergeant and was very helpful to the young officers. We had now returned to Dinapur and Walters was brought before the C.O. for the usual offence and was about to be severely punished but I asked the C.O. to give Walters one more chance and said I would guarantee his behaviour. The C.O. who was a very kindly man, reluctantly agreed, and I put Walters in charge of the Company stores – armament, ammunition, bedding, etc. Since it was Christmas time the Regimental contractor, Mohamed Amin, had sent every company a small barrel of beer which were put in the Company Stores. Next morning the Company Sergeant Major went into the Stores and found four prostrate figures – including Walters – and an empty barrel of beer. The Colonel never let me forget it. The last time I met Walters he was a warden in St. James's Park. We left the swans and the ducks and went to the nearest pub to celebrate.

In the extremely humid weather in the months preceding the Monsoon, British troops and their families were moved to various hill stations, half of the troops remaining behind for security reasons. The troops mostly got prickly heat, which was most uncomfortable, whilst the "hot weather bird" with its horrible chirp kept one awake. However, "C" company's turn arrived in 1932 and we went to a station near Darjeeling Jallapakar, higher up than Darjeeling, and on a clear evening one had a beautiful view of Kinchinjunga and the three pinnacles of Everest. Higher still were the remains of an old outpost position, probably from during the Afghan Wars when the small garrison was so depressed at living perpetually in the clouds that, with their officer, they decided to jump off the top of the cliff together.

I very much wanted to shoot a tiger, and a friend of mine, with a vast estate in North Bihar, invited me to stay a few days and he would give me the opportunity. He knew there was a large tiger, feared by the native villagers, in the area. He accordingly tethered a buffalo as bait and constructed a small *machan* (a few planks in a tree) about ten feet up, and gave me a rifle. It was a moonlit night and a few hours later the tiger arrived and pounced on the buffalo. Hearing or scenting me, he opened his jaws to attack! With trembling hands I pressed the trigger and shot him. As I write, his head is just behind me with open jaws and a ferocious look, just as he was when I shot him. He was one of the world's largest recorded tigers ever to be shot.

My tiger.

It was here that I received my notification that I had passed into the Staff College at Quetta in Baluchistan and was to experience two very tough but extremely interesting years. In November 1932 I married the elder daughter of the Commandant, (later) General Sir Roger Wilson. We left just before the Quetta earthquake, feeling the effects of it at Delhi, several hundred miles away.

Coastal Command – R.A.F.

On returning to England from India with my newly wedded wife, in January 1935, I was posted to the 1st Battalion of my Regiment at Shorncliffe. Having come straight from the Staff College at Quetta, I was mostly employed on training exercises and umpiring on manoeuvres. It was very depressing that the Battalion had only 400 other ranks instead of 808 and on manoeuvres a number of platoons and other sub-units were represented by green flags. I can see the cynical smile on the German Military attaché's face as the Battalion marched past the General commanding Southern Command.

In about March 1936, I was posted as Organisation Officer to No. 1 Bomber Group R.A.F. at Abingdon. The Group comprised six stations of two squadrons each. The Group was mostly equipped with Hinds and Harts, completely out of date, and only two seaters with a small bomb load. Some months later we joyously heard that we were to get two war winners, Battles and Blenheims. They were bigger and faster but not up to the standard required. In fact, in their second engagement in France, the Bosche shot down a whole squadron of Battles: the Blenheims lasted a little longer.

At the end of a year I was sent back to the Army and posted as Brigade Major 2nd London Infantry Brigade, T.A. at Armoury House. The Brigade were the well known Gray Brigade. The H.A.C., London Scottish, London Rifle Brigade, Queens, Westminster, Q.V.R. and the Kensingtons. With the threatening war clouds recruits flocked in their hundreds, mostly from the City. Most weekends I laid on a tactical exercise for officers and in August we camped at Burley in Hampshire. Here we carried out a realistic exercise. I arranged with Tidworth to send down enough lorries to embuss a brigade and I arranged with the nearest R.A.F. station to come and bomb the brigade with smoke bombs as they were debussing – and before it carried out an attack.

The famous military historian, Liddel Hart, was most impressed and we lunched together in London and discussed the strategy, factors and weaponry of the next war and his ideas, particularly on tank and anti-tank defence, but we disagreed on the role of the infantry.

It was about this time that the Prime Minister, Sir Neville Chamberlain, returned from the meeting with Hitler at Munich and proclaimed "Peace in our time with honour," and everybody was joyful and understandably relieved. My Brigadier took me to lunch at the Trocadero where the band played patriotic music and everybody cheered. Shortly afterwards, I returned to the R.A.F. as Wing Commander Org. Coastal Command at Lee-on-Solent and then at Northwood – a most unusual job for a soldier to organise aircraft that flew over the sea. However, owing to the considerable expansion of the R.A.F., flying officers could not be spared for staff duties and the War Office agreed to loan them a few staff officers.

Coastal Command (which eventually was taken over by the Royal Navy) covered the whole of the British Isles from the Shetlands to Cornwall and Ulster. Its primary tasks were to protect our shipping from the submarine menace and also to shadow German ships in the North Sea. The most important strategical area was the vital bottle-neck between the Shetlands and Iceland. The Royal Navy sent a strong flotilla of cruisers, destroyers, etc. to Sullum Voe on the North-west coast of the Shetlands. Our great Commander-in-Chief, affectionately known as Ginger Bowhill, decided to send two squadrons of Sunderlands, an excellent and spacious flying boat, and also an old passenger ship, S.S. *Manela,* was commandeered to provide accommodation and a base for the crews of the flying boat squadron. A few days later I received a communication from the Wing Commander of the flying boats to the effect that the sailors had been wonderfully hospitable and every night officers and O.R.s had been invited on board one warship or another where their gin was only twopence a tot while the *Manela's* crew had to pay shore prices. I immediately took it up with the R.A.F. H.Q. in Kingsway, London, who referred it to the Customs & Excise who refused to consider it – whereupon I went up to London and stormed into my opposite number at R.A.F. H.Q. and he rang up the Customs & Excise who then ordained that if the S.S. *Manela* went to a foreign port and returned she would qualify for alcohol at naval rates. S.S. *Manela* accordingly sailed to Gibraltar at full speed and returned to Sullum Voe but the festivities were not to last long. This sounds, of course, a ridiculous story but I have no doubt that records could confirm this.

Ginger Bowhill learnt that Sunderlands unfortunately had not the range to cover the sea passage between the Shetlands and Iceland. About this time, however, the Americans sent us a specimen of their new flying boat, a Catalina, which had a longer range than the Sunderlands. Our commander was delighted and he decided to try it out on a trip to Iceland. Unfortunately, Iceland, being a neutral country, interned the Catalina and its crew. However, the Icelanders relented and the Catalina returned.

One day I was sent up to the Shetlands to look for a possible landing strip near Lerwick, the capital of the Shetlands, and we found an excellent site which was very useful later. Incidentally, the first bomb of the war was dropped on the Shetlands and I understand that the sole casualty was a rabbit. A rather amusing incident concerns a German with ginger hair who lived in Lerwick for some months, and was very popular with the Lerwickians, but he left just before the war; later a German aeroplane flew just above several roof tops over Lerwick and its pilot was recognised as "Ginger Fritz" and they all waved to him. Obviously he had been a planted spy.

The A.O.C. in Chief was becoming very anxious about the number of serviceable aircraft and crew in all stations and I have in front of me the consolidated report of the issue on the outbreak of war. Some squadrons only had two or three serviceable aircraft; others were nearer establishment but short of crew; one, in Ulster, where two squadrons of American long-distance bombers had arrived which had no wirelesses or bomb-racks, and so on – what a deplorable situation at that late hour!

I was again sent up to Scotland and the Shetlands and on returning on or about August 31st in the evening, flying above the clouds, there was a brilliant setting sun casting rays over the clouds which from above looked like a pink carpet.

Ginger Bowhill was particularly anxious that I should visit Leuchars on the Aberdeen coast and the base of two R.A.F.V.R. land-based squadrons, one equipped with Ansons and the other with Hudsons. Ansons were a very reliable aircraft but lacking in speed, Hudsons, an American aircraft, were small but very effective, but tragically seven or eight young pilots were killed owing to engine failure shortly after take off. Understandably, the morale of the squadron was badly affected and so Hudson crews were flown to America where apparently the reason for these tragic accidents was explained and rectified. Later in the war, I frequently travelled in Hudsons but was always relieved when I disembarked. And so I reached Invergordon. I was in a flying boat but Leuchar was land-based and I had to transfer to a Fleet Air Arm plane, piloted by a very young officer. It was hellishly foggy (the lovely pink carpet I had been flying over!). The fog got worse and worse and we decided to return and as the pilot turned, to our horror we were confronted by the top of a steep cliff: the pilot, just in time, in a split second, was able to skim over it! We were both very near the end of our existence here on earth.

At Invergordon a message was awaiting me to return to Northwood and I was taken by car to a main line station just in time to catch the London train. I sat down in a carriage and a policeman came in to tell me that the carriage was reserved and, as I was leaving, I was confronted with Sir Neville and Lady Chamberlain, their holiday having been interrupted by events. I duly reported at Northwood and arranged for a bed to be set up in my office for the next few critical days: a wise move as the timing of the following urgent message from the Air Ministry confirmed and from which I quote an extract.

Date 3.9.39   Time 0215
"The British Government will present an ultimatum to Germany on Thursday, 3rd September, unless compliance with the ultimatum is received by 11.00 p.m. we shall be at War."

There followed my mobilisation orders. Next morning, just before 1100 hours, all officers assembled in the ante-room and when the hour struck our Commander-in-Chief announced that we had now declared war on Germany and that all units of Coastal Command were at Action Stations.

War

A few days later I was again sent up to Scotland and with Group Captain Gould, who was the Chief Engineer of the Command, went to the Flying Boat Reserve station at Calshot on Southampton Water and we then proceeded on to Scotland in an antediluvian flying boat, the London, maximum speed 90 knots. At this time solitary German marauding aircraft had shot down some of our flying boats over sea and land. The weather was stormy and we were passing the island of Hoy when suddenly the engines of the London started to rev- up and the London turned over on its side and started to descend towards the sea. I went up to the cockpit and the pilot pointed towards the sea where a German U-boat was submerging and he told me he was about drop our two 250-lb. bombs. Naturally, Gould and I felt much happier for we thought we had had it. However, we watched the bombs descend but they were a long way off target. We eventually returned to Northwood. I now had two more officers on my staff and there was tremendous activity.

Before concluding I must mention the "nerve centre" of Coastal Command, namely, the Operation Room. It was a very large room (probably the vaults of the former hotel). On the front wall was an enormous map covering the seas around Great Britain from the Baltic to Iceland and far into the Atlantic. On it, on information from our flying boats, the Admiralty and other sources were able to pinpoint the known location of German warships, U-boats and, on occasions, movements of our own Navy. Of course the whole picture was continually changing as further information came in and the changes were marked on the map by the W.R.A.F. Of course there was a very up-to-date signals and W/T office. It was always fascinating to go into the Op. Room for a few minutes – but never more so than the dramatic episode of the *Altmark*.

In both World Wars the Germans had considerable naval forces in the South Atlantic; being on many trade routes it was a profitable hunting ground. One can remember the not very successful battle of the Falklands in World War I and the *Graf Spee* in World War II. To sustain their presence so far from Europe they had supply ships of which one was the *Altmark*. Of course they were ordinary merchant ships and avoided suspicion. S.S. *Altmark*, having emptied her supplies, was ordered to collect a large number of the captives from ships which had been sunk. They were crammed into the holds. I don't know what ensign she was flying but information had been received of her human cargo. Some destroyers, Under Admiral Vian, were at the ready and followed *Altmark* into a Narvik Norwegian fjord, went alongside, boarded her and opened the holds and the prisoners yelled with joy, "The Navy's here!" We, in the Ops. Room likewise cheered.

Four Naval Captains in uniform (including an M.P.) were at Northwood as liaison officers with the Admiralty and there was a certain amount of mutual antagonism between the two services. The sailors would come in to see me as a soldier and complain these "something" airmen knew nothing about the war at sea. Shortly after, an R.A.F. officer would come in with the reverse complaint that the "something" sailors knew nothing about war in the air. In both cases, as a simple soldier, I tactfully agreed with them.

Another incident at that time was concerning the magnetic mine which was another sinister device produced by the Germans – the object of which was to be exploded magnetically by ships passing above it. A few of these mines had been laid near the estuary of the Thames and a quick decision was necessary to see if they could be exploded from an aircraft filled with the appropriate apparatus. Two young pilot officers were detailed for this hazardous experiment and one of them came to my office to tell me that he did not wish to take on this job. However, by telling him that it was his duty to obey an order, I soon talked him over and his mission was successful. He exploded the mine which shook his plane but he landed safely and was awarded an A.F.C. A naval friend of mine, Commander Ouvrie, defused one mine which was left ashore at low tide and obtained other valuable information – at great risk to his life and for this he was awarded a D.S.O.

This has been a somewhat sombre recitation of my nine months with Coastal Command. But there were amusing incidents of which I will quote one. Just before war was declared, His Majesty King George VI visited Northwood. We were assembled in the anteroom and were introduced to His Majesty and then went into the dining-room for tea. At the table I was seated opposite His Majesty. I rarely wore my Sam Browne belt except on special occasions. Hearing of His Majesty's visit I went to my home and polished up the leather and brass on the belt. Whilst we were having our tea party, His Majesty looked at me and asked me why I was wearing the cross belt of my Sam Browne. I stammered something about it being part of my military uniform, whereupon he asked if I had read his orders to which I responded in the negative. "Didn't the War Office inform you that in order to economise on leather, of which there is a great shortage, I issued this order?" I again answered in the negative, whereupon His Majesty turned to Ginger Bowhill, saying, "Just like the War Office who never seem to read my orders." Needless to say the thirty or so officers in their blue uniforms were delighted to hear the "Royal Raspberry" to the only one in khaki.

And so I end my recording of my nine months service which I would not have missed for the world with Coastal Command. Of course, in the phoney war period from the outbreak of war until Dunkirk, it was the only R.A.F. command continually on active service. Bomber and Fighter command became predominant later. I was proud to have served under the Air Chief Marshal, Sir Frederick Bowhill, and grateful to him for recommending me for the Order of the British Empire which I was awarded in the King's Birthday honours.

Ulster, 1940 - 1941

On leaving Coastal Command, I was posted to command a newly formed Territorial Battalion, the 6th Royal Berkshires at Southampton. The Companies were billetted in schools and other buildings; the mess and headquarters at King Edward's School and the officers in the Polygon Hotel. Shortly after the "phoney war" ended and the Dunkirk evacuation was imminent a Brigade of Regular and T.A. Rifle Regiments passed through Southampton. I met many old Rifle officers whom I knew in the Polygon Bar and they all seemed in very good heart. The object of the Brigade was to go to Calais as a decoy and to attract German bombers from the Dunkirk evacuation. They duly embarked on two large transports. Arriving at Calais harbour the situation was so critical they had to disembark with only their small arms and the bombing of the harbour was so intense that the transports had to leave and return to Southampton.

The local district Commander rang me up in the early morning and told me to send two Companies immediately to unload the two transports as the dockers had refused to do so "without receiving danger money!" The troops unloaded the transports with astonishing rapidity, putting all the kits and personal possessions aside. Since the troops had not yet been equipped with modern weapons they were, for the first time during the next few days, able to practise with them on Southampton Common where young soldiers learned to drive carriers, set up mortars, machine guns, etc., but Southern Command send down lorries to collect them all. Our Quartermaster, Pat Twynam, was a shrewd and far-seeing chap and he managed to conceal many thousands of rounds of small arms ammunition. To revert to the Calais Rifle Battalion, they had put up a gallant fight but all were killed or captured but undoubtedly served their purpose in diverting a massive air bombardment at Dunkirk.

An obstacle course.

Carrier crossing trench.

A few days later the 1st Division was ordered to proceed to Ulster immediately. At that time, after Dunkirk and the invasion of France, there was a distinct possibility that the Germans would land in Ireland. There was a German Embassy in Dublin and many of the Irish citizens were pro-German. Accordingly the 6th Battalion entrained at Southampton, embarked at Stranraer, disembarked at Larne and marched to Kilwaughter to a camp in the grounds of an ancient castle.

For the next few weeks I set about reorganising the battalion, i.e. the formation of a carrier platoon, a signal section, a mortar section, an intelligence section and a fighting patrol (an idea of my own which paid dividends later).

Many officers of the Battalion thought it would be a splendid idea to get a brass band. Accordingly, I contacted the Regimental Depot at Reading and, in due course, band instruments and an excellent band-master arrived. It was a great boost to the morale of the troops, especially when meeting them and leading them for the last mile of their long marches and on ceremonial occasions it was most effective. Contrary to War Office orders abolishing compulsory Church Parades, I decided that every Sunday morning we would have a Church Parade, Company Commanders letting off those with reasonable excuses. Both at Larne and Coleraine the local vicars were most co-operative. These parades were very impressive, particularly at Coleraine. The Battalion would parade in line, I would arrive, they would be called to attention and there would not be movement of an eyebrow. I would then lead them to Church where I would read the lesson and, at the end of the service, I would proceed to the centre of the bridge and, led by the band, the Companies, one by one, would march past me. As they approached the bridge the band would play the Regimental march, followed by that old tune "The Farmer's Boy," which incidentally was the Battalion's "code name" and once more I say that they marched past like Guardsmen. Usually an empty coach was awaiting to take them to their girl friends in Larne.

At Kilwaughter, in the summer we usually held our Church service in the open. On one such occasion, the Larne Home Guard (the Constabulary) rang up to ask if they might attend and at the end of the service two of them marched forward and presented us with a very large shelalagh (an Irish club), together with a green riband, showing their appreciation of the help we had given them. It hangs in my front hall, near my General Strike truncheon, and woe betide the burglar should one try to break in!

I have perhaps over extended my reports on Church parades and bands but I do feel they both contributed to a large extent to the wonderful spirit of the Battalion at that time.

We were now fully equipped with modern armament and fortunately we were near a locality which, with a steep hill in the background and moorland in the foreground, formed a most natural field firing range, and supported by our affiliated Royal Artillery battery (armed with World War I French guns) each Company in turn had to carry out a most realistic and somewhat dangerous attack. (One or two of our chaps were slightly wounded). We had other minor exercises, our own troops providing the oppositon forces, hence only blank ammunition was to be fired. In a final exercise A Company carried out an attack in which a flock of sheep were grazing between A Company and the "enemy" when suddenly a sheep fell dead. I was extremely angry for someone had fired a live round and compensation had to be paid to the farmer. The next day the Battalion left Kilwaughter and were encamped or billetted in Larne, about 2 miles away. A Company decided to hold a party in a local hall, to which I was invited. One of the items was a raffle draw and, out of courtesy to their C.O. I was asked to draw ticket no. 1. A few minutes afterwards. Captain Trimmer, the Company Commander, announced that the winner was ticket no. 1, Lt. Col. K. P. Smith, and midst great applause, I went up to receive my prize – when four men appeared carrying a dead sheep. My extreme anger suddenly turned to merriment and I hoped that A Company would, at the time of severe rationing, enjoy their mutton for the next few days – but I never knew the chap who fired that live round!

We had been at Kilwaughter and Larne about 11 months and the Battalion was now an organised and fighting unit. The citizens of Larne were very friendly and a few of our men actually married Larne girls. We then moved to Coleraine in the North of Ulster on the River Bann, with one Company at Port Stuart and the remainder of the Battalion accommodated in a large Irish linen factory in which sleeping quarters for 600 men, kitchens and sanitary requirements had been constructed. The Officers Mess and sleeping quarters were in a large country house on slightly higher ground and with about 20 acres of ground at our disposal, which we made excellent use of by forming our own battle school, digging trenches, barbed wire entanglements, booby traps, etc. Our pioneer section had devised a superstructure, which could be put on (and taken off) a carrier, to make it resemble a tank – a most ingenious and useful idea.

My Intelligence Officer, Tony Greenly, wrote a short history of the Battalion in Ulster. Also, in a large album, he inserted many photographs of individuals and the general activities of the Battalion, from which I reproduce the five photographs in this chapter.

Our Intelligence Section was both lively and extremely enterprising. One day, I think it was Tony's successor, asked me if he could take his section into the wilderness for a few days; I agreed, provided he told me where I could find him. I eventually found him and his section in a hay loft. Amongst their exploits was to get into the offices of the Admiralty in Londonderry and come away with some non-confidential documents without being challenged, which of course were later returned.

Occasionally I held a "T.E.W.T." (Tactical exercise without troops) and I concocted "Exercise Dynamite" in which Lieut. Dynamite dreamed a dream that he had left Ulster and was now at war. He was sent out with a fighting patrol in which he was confronted with ten critical situations, all of which he successfully dealt with, and on return was presented with a Military Cross by his C.O.

Scene I   Lieut. Dynamite on a camp bed in the mess, having his restless dream.

Scene II   Lieut. Dynamite, having successfully completed his ten skirmishes returned and was presented with his M.C.

However, I divided the officers into syndicates and they had to solve Dynamite's 10 problems – such as if you were attacked by an enemy patrol over there how would you deal with it? Supposing the enemy were in that house how would you attack it? If you had to cross that bridge with an enemy pillbox, how would you set about it? The Officers all enjoyed it and, indeed, it was a very useful exercise.

Scene III   Back in the Mess, Dynamite woke up and, with horror, sees his C.O. asking him why he was not on parade!

By that time our exercises were at Brigade and Divisional levels. The other two Battalions of 184 Brigade were the Oxford, Buckinghamshire Light Infantry and the Buckinghamshire Battalion with whom we were on very friendly terms.

We also maintained close contact with the Ulster Special Constabulary who were the local Home Guard and they asked if they might take part in some of our exercises. I remember on one occasion when a section of them were occupying a defensive position by the side of a small road, pointing out that their Bren gun was pointing in the wrong direction, "If the Germans came round that corner," and was abruptly interrupted, "Ach, it isn't the Germans we're waiting for," said they – and so it is today and has been from Cromwell's battle of the Boyne.

By now 6th Battalion had become renowned for its bellicosity. And now our last battle: I cannot remember the full details of the occasion but we were to be attacked by another Brigade of the Division and I sent forth my carrier platoon, fighter patrol and, possibly, a Company to deal with them. Within half an hour or so, escorted prisoners were trickling in and as they arrived were pushed into a large wooden barn by Major James Coker and other stalwarts until the barn contained between 100 and 180 prisoners, rather reminding me of the "the Black Hole of Calcutta" in Clive's days. Also, six armoured cars of the North Irish Horse arrived, which I compounded nearby in a small field with their crews. Whilst I was considering what to do next the armoured cars revved up and started to leave the compound. In my anger I hurled my precious Dunhill pipe (which I had recently bought in London for £14) at the leading armoured car. However, despite the loss of my Dunhill, it was a "famous victory."

My last gruelling test for the Battalion was to order every company in turn to carry out a fifty mile march across country without transport and carrying their arms and equipment – within 24 hours. Every company completed its task: A Company in 19 hours, a remarkable achievement. On its return each company was met by the band. Likewise, I met them and was immensely proud of them – almost to tears. At that time all letters had to be vetted and I was delighted to read some of their cheerful letters to their families at home about the march.

Unexpectedly, we were ordered to march to Londonderry. Apparently a German bomb had destroyed a cargo load of Scotch whisky which was destined for America in part repayment of our War Debt

Attack through smoke.

Carrier platoon training.

and future supplies would be consigned to the linen factory at Coleraine. Before we departed, the local Mayor and Council invited our officers to a farewell party. In his speech the Mayor likened the 6th Battalion to the Australian soldiers and their "devil may care" spirit but also to the Guards, with their smartness and discipline. What a wonderful tribute!

We duly marched to Londonderry. The Officers Mess and accommodation was in a large house with a long drive up to it. The Brigadier called a meeting of his three C.O.s and whilst there the telephone rang from the War Office who said that I had been appointed to command the First Malta Brigade. Naturally, I was elated, being a Regular Soldier, but at the same time sad at leaving my beloved Battalion. In this context I would mention the Officers Mess Sergeant, H. L. Smith, and Private Hopkins, my servant, who on suspecting me of having a cold ordered me to bed – and then shortly afterwards a tap at the door and they entered with a glass of "hot tonic" and, assuredly, I was better the next day; also my driver, Private Dovey, who in my cross country ventures on foot would always be at the right spot at the right time to pick me up. I would also pay tribute to the citizens of Ulster for their kindness. In those days there were few signs of religious animosity. Finally, a word for our Divisional Commander, Major General Carton de Wiart, V.C., later General Sir Adrian Carton de Wiart. He had been wounded thirteen times and lost his left arm and an eye. He was always interested in our exercises and we all loved him.

But the sad day had come. A farewell lunch party was held in he mess and, afterwards, I shook hands with all the officers in the hall and, on leaving, was surprised to see my car with Private Dovey at the wheel. Then I noted that the Warrant Officers and Sergeants of the Battalion were holding ropes attached to the car and the band was in front with 800 men of the Battalion lined up each side of the drive. The band was playing my favourite march, the cortège moved slowly up the drive – the saddest five minutes of my life. My sentiments are epitomised in my farewell message – again extracted from Tony Greenly's album:–

> "I will always regard 2nd December, 1941 as the saddest day of my life. After twenty months I have relinquished command of a body of men who had become very dear to me. I took the Battalion over, owing to force of circumstances, as a partially

trained body. I leave it as a Battalion whose efficiency and spirit cannot be beaten in the British Army. As a regular soldier I have possibly aimed sometimes at a very high standard. It was my job to do so. But no amount of drive can produce the required results unless the men respond, and you have all done so in a manner which has excited the admiration of everyone who has ever made contact with the Battalion.

I thank you from the bottom of my heart for your understanding, your fortitude, your discipline and the wonderful pride in

Gen. Carton de Wiart.

your Battalion. My one regret is that I won't be commanding you when you first meet the "Hun." Because I know you will acquit yourselves like men when the occasion arises.

I would like to have said farewell personally to every Warrant Officer, N.C.O. and man in the Battalion. As I left the camp I saw many old faces I would love to have had one last word with, one last shake of the hand, but it couldn't be done and I hope those concerned will understand.

May God bless you all. May He give you fortitude through the stormy years that lie ahead and may He bring you back safe again to your homes when it is all over."

Before ending my Ulster saga, I may have given the impression that those 20 months were never ending, tough training, but far from it, we had our fun and games. Before leaving Kilwaughter on the 60th Anniversary of the Royal Berkshires' most famous battle of Maiwand in Afghanistan, where the eleven survivors of the forward companies, sooner than surrender to the Afghan army, charged with fixed bayonets to their death. The only survivor was a soldier's dog, "Bobby," who got back in the ghastly retreat of certain Indian Regiments and the surviving members of the rear companies of the 66th to Kandahar. Shortly afterwards, Lord Roberts, in his famous march from Kabul to Kandahar, relieved the beleagured garrison. Eventually, remnants of the 66th returned to the U.K. and were stationed at Newport barracks on the Isle of wight. Queen Victoria, at Osborne House, sent for "Bobby" who was taken there by a soldier in full dress and she decorated "Bobby" with the Afghan war medal. "Bobby" can still be seen in a glass case in the museum of the Duke of Edinburgh's Royal Regiment (Berkshires and Wiltshires) in the Cathedral Close, Salisbury.

Thus, whilst at Kilwaughter on Maiwand Day, we had a celebration in the grounds of the castle, the chief item being a competition for the most amusing or impressive turn-out either on a vehicle or a horse. The contestants all assembled near the castle and while the band played, they passed the judges one by one. In the old coach house of the castle a four-wheeled gilded carriage had been found (rather like the Royal Coach) and this led the parade; sitting inside was Lord Kilwaughter with an enormous white beard; then came "Lady Godiva" wearing pants and carrying a parasol, seated on a horse.

Other vehicles followed and the most impressive was a group of an officer and ten men, standing motionless as in the famous picture of that historic battle on 27th July 1880 – but it lacked a "Bobby."

We also had concert parties in which the actors were born comedians and one with a beautiful tenor voice. Even at Coleraine we had an Officers Ball which, with our own band and no charge from the Town Hall, cost very little but was great fun.

I subsequently commanded two famous Regular Brigades which, besides heavy casualties, were still magnificent troops and, in fact, both Brigades landed on D-Day, 1944, but magnificent as they were, it was entirely due to the reputation of the 6th Battalion that I was selected to command these two Brigades. As I said in my farewell message, "No amount of drive can produce the desired results unless the men willingly respond" – and this they did!

On our very last exercise, defending the crossings over a river, we eventually retired and were resting near a small village. Some of us went into a church and were confronted with a large marble replica of the famous picture of the battle of Maiwand. Underneath was an incription, "Here lieth the body of Lt. Col. J. Galbraith, the Commanding Officer of the 66th Regiment, who was killed at the battle of Maiwand, 27th July 1880" – an extraordinary coincidence so soon after our Maiwand celebration at Kilwaughter.

After I had left the Battalion the 61st Division moved to England under a new Divisional Commander, but unfortunately it became a reinforcement division. Of course, most of the 6th Battalion, officers and other ranks, went overseas and were posted to many other regiments (one draft to a Highland Battalion where they had to wear kilts!).

After failing to take Caen on D-Day, as I was awaiting the aeroplane to fly me home, I received a message from the Reinforcement Depot with a list of one officer and 36 other ranks: "We, the undersigned, who served in the 6th Royal Berkshire Regiment, have been posted to 3rd Division and wish to serve in a Battalion of your Brigade." Sadly, at that late hour I could take no action.

As was to be expected, many of the 6th Battalion officers and O.R.s never came home. For forty-three years the officers of the Battalion have had a reunion dinner in London but "Anno Dominae" takes its toll, but the spirit of the 6th Royal Berkshires will go on for ever.

The Siege of Malta, 1941 - 43

Part I – The Voyage

Whilst commanding the 6th Royal Berkshires in Ulster, I received a letter from the War Office informing me that I was under consideration for command of the 1st Parachute Brigade and that, as I should be expected to perform certain unusual duties, I could refuse the offer of this appointment without prejudice to my military career. I accepted this offer, which had also been sent to a Guards officer, who had refused, and to Lt. Col. Richard Gale, commanding a Worcestershire Battalion. After a sleepless night, for he was a hefty man and didn't like the idea of jumping out of an aeroplane, he rang up the War Office and accepted. Actually, the War Office decided that Brigade Commanders should not jump, and later General Sir Richard Gale, as he became, commanded the 6th Airborne Division on D-Day, with great distinction.

I was naturally disappointed and a few days later I received a message from the War Office informing me that I had been appointed to command the 1st Malta Brigade. Again I was upset for I had, for the past 18 months, been training my Battalion in mobile warfare and, moreover, the bombing of Malta was daily news. So I went to the Military Secretary who told me that I had been selected from the twelfth down the list of potential Brigadiers because now that the Italians had joined the Germans, Malta was of vital strategic importance as it controlled the central Mediterranean and the supply lines to General Rommel. I was told to report to H.M.S. *Nestor* at Grennock on the Clyde. After a few days leave I reported to Commander Rosenthal who told me that he would take me to Gibraltar.

H.M.S. *Nestor* was a new Australian destroyer with an Aussie crew. With three other destroyers, and later joined by four very obsolete American destroyers, we were escorting an enormous convoy carrying a whole division of troops with their full equipment and armament, bound for the Middle East. We sailed off down the Clyde and joined the convoy which was a most impressive sight, ships as far as one could see. The American destroyers joined us off Londonderry but it soon became obvious that we were in for a very rough voyage. In fact, the American destroyers, with their tall funnels, could not compete with the mountainous waves and returned to Londonderry. I had the Captain's cabin, as during the voyage he could not leave the bridge. I was unable to rest on the Captain's bed and so dragged his mattress on to the floor on which I had to lie in spreadeagled fashion for the cabin was above the propeller and every time the *Nestor* dived down an enormous wave the whole stern shuddered.

Suddenly, the *Nestor's* guns started firing and the alarm bell went, and as the cabin doors would automatically close, I went up to the bridge where the Captain pointed out a fast moving light in the scudding clouds. At that time long-distance German aircraft were frequently attacking our ships and contacting their submarines. The navigating officer then told Rosenthal he thought that the light was a star, probably Venus. Then the Commodore of the convoy, a retired Admiral, signalled Rosenthal, asking at what he was firing? "At Venus," the latter replied, and the Admiral replied, "Bad luck! She was a luscious lady but only had one arm (*vide* the famous Venus de Milo statue) and wouldn't be much good!"

For the next few days the weather was tempestuous. This convoy had to go far into the Atlantic on its voyage to the Cape. My meals were brought by the Captain's servant, Ford, a delightful chap, but I am afraid that my *mal de mer* had curtailed my appetite. I often popped into the wardroom for a chat with the Australian officers and one night we heard the tragic news that the British battleships *The Prince of Wales* and *Renown* had been sunk by the Japs off Singapore, which distressed the Aussies as it was too near their homeland.

Every now and again there would be a submarine alarm. "Action Stations" would sound and star-shells were fired which illuminated the convoy area. In three days the stormy weather abated and our destroyers were relieved by four destroyers from Gibraltar. The next morning I was awakened by "Action Stations," went up to the bridge and witnessed a most inspiring sight – the four destroyers in line at 32 knots, all firing their forward guns. Rosenthal told me that a German submarine had been sighted. I stood beside the Captain on the bridge and, having reached the spot, the asdic-hydrophone recorded that we were near the submarine, so we dropped five depth charges; but the

Depth charge exploding such as the one dropped by H.M.S. "Nestor" when she sank a German submarine.

asdic ceased to function and Rosenthal assumed that the submarine had escaped and so ordered the other destroyers to follow *Nestor's* line ahead to Gibraltar. Suddenly, H.M.S. *Croome* signalled that wreckage was coming to the surface, so *Nestor* returned and, sure enough, it was in considerable quantity. A whale boat was launched and the wreckage collected, including garments made in Berlin and part of a human arm, woodwork, and so on, but the most significant was a large patch of oil. The wreckage was laid out on my cabin table and we reached Gibraltar on December 16th. Admiral Somerville, Commander in Chief, Mediterranean Fleet, came aboard, closely inspected the wreckage and congratulated Commander Rosenthal on his success.

Disembarking at Gibraltar, I bade farewell to Rosenthal, his officers and crew. The Aussies of all ranks could not have been more friendly, despite my being a mere "pongo"! I was met by a Staff Officer who took me up the Rock to a villa where he was billeted and in the afternoon was taken round the Rock and the lengthy tunnels which formed part of the fortress and met the Governor-General, Lord Gort, V.C., who was extremely interesting. Gibraltar, of course, is the door to the Mediterranean and Hitler was inciting Franco to invade it, but fortunately, he was not keen to do so for it would have brought Spain into the war. Meanwhile, the R.A.F. arranged for a Beaufighter (a night fighter), piloted by Wing Commander Stainforth (who, with his brother, had won the Schneider Cup) to take me to Malta. Arriving at Luqa aerodrome, I was met by Brigadier D. O'Donovan, from whom I was to take over the Brigade, and escorted to the Mess and introduced to my Staff.

Part II – The Siege

Many accounts of this historic siege have been published and this account, based on my own personal experiences, does not pay adequate tribute to the three Armed Services nor to the chief victims, the Maltese themselves. To quote an ancient adage, "By uniting we stand, by dividing we fall" – and thus Malta did not fall.

Brigadier O'Donovan, who was a very pleasant man, took me round, introducing me to General Scobell (an old family friend), to the Naval and R.A.F. commanders, to the Deputy Governor, Sir Edward Jackson and to H.E. The Governor and Commander in Chief, General Dobbie and to C.O.s of my Brigade, i.e. 1st Dorset, 2nd Devons and 1st Hampshire Regiments, all of whom were regular soldiers and had been in the Middle East for many years. I had also the 3rd Kings Own Malta battalion.

I was very impressed with the historic fortress, its ancient palaces of the Knights of St. John and its magnificent harbour, in which Nelson, after the battle of the Nile, captured the remnants of the French fleet and, much to the joy of the islanders, Malta became part of the British Empire. After putting me in the picture, Brigadier O'Donovan returned to England. I remember that on his last evening some bombs were dropped very close to us. At that time three or four raids took place every day.

Early in the year 1941, when Mussolini joined the Axis, Italian bombers, flying at great height, began the bombing of Malta. We had a few A.A. guns but no R.A.F. squadrons. On the quayside were three obsolete Gloucester Gladiators destined for Egypt. There happened to be four R.A.F. Staff Officers on a mission on the island. They got the three Gladiators out of their crates and up they went to meet the Wops (Italians), who were petrified and avoided contact. Our three planes, nicknamed Faith, Hope and Charity, became heroes in the eyes of the Maltese. They shot one or two Wop planes down and achieved their object in keeping the enemy well up in the heavens. Later on, about June 1941, a large convoy, escorted by the aircraft carrier H.M.S. *Illustrious,* was passing through the Mediterranean to Alexandria and Hitler ordered the German Air Marshal, Kesserling, to attack her and the convoy, which he endeavoured to do. The *Illustrious* was hit three times and forced to enter Valetta for urgent repairs. The Luftwaffe came over in tremendous strength in wave after wave. A smokescreen covered the harbour and the *Illustrious* escaped further damage but the surrounding houses, particularly in the Eastern part of the Grand Harbour, known as the "Three Cities," were flattened. Happily, *Illustrious* was made seaworthy in remarkably quick time, quitted Valetta in darkness and reached Alexandria. Kesserling and his Luftwaffe were ordered back to the Russian front.

This all happened some six or seven months before I arrived. By now the Huns had overrun Europe and Great Britain was herself in danger of invasion. But in Malta, *Illustrious's* incident was long ago and I found that a sort of euphoria had set in, so far away from the war. Lunch parties in the Union Club and dinner parties galore – and I regret that the same spirit had penetrated the whole island, including the garrisons, which had recently been reinforced by more R.A.F. fighters and bombers, A.A. gunners, etc. to make Malta well nigh impregnable. Since Nelson, there was usually a powerful flotilla of warships in the Grand Harbour. Our submarines were actively engaged in attacking Axis merchant ships loaded with arms, ammunition and other essentials of war destined for General Rommel. Sadly, their casualty list was alarmingly high; so many of these gallant mariners never returned, one of the Commanders being awarded a posthumous V.C. However, they sank an incredible number of Axis ships which was the prime reason for Hitler's determination to capture Malta.

The ground defence policy was purely static. Around the coast and aerodromes in some depth were situated concrete pillboxes, about 300 – 400 yards apart, supplemented by a continuous belt of wire and land mines. Each pillbox was garrisoned by a section of eight or so men with Bren guns and other weapons. Undoubtedly they would have presented considerable opposition and inflicted many casualties but smoke and modern weapons would have defeated them, so I gave orders that slit trenches were to be dug outside every pillbox. The troops had even made little gardens and some even kept hens! One day my Brigade Major, Paul Atkins, and I visited seven unoccupied pillboxes and collected seven Bren guns. I quote this incident to demonstrate how tragically unaware the infantry were of the perilous situation in which Malta would soon find itself.

The WOPs came over most days and scattered their bombs over the countryside. A few JU.88's came over three or four times but they were bombing justifiable targets – the harbour or aerodromes. But the palmy days Malta had been enjoying were soon to come to an abrupt end. Kesserling, with a more powerful Luftwaffe, had returned to Sardinia and Sicily with orders from Hitler to destroy the defences of Malta preparatory to an invasion by sea and air.

About this time Major General Daniel Beak, V.C., D.S.O., M.C. had taken over from General Scobell. He was a difficult man but a terrific "fire-eater," and thoroughly agreed with my emphasis on mobility. I have in front of me the Axis proposed plan of invasion. Approximately two seaborne divisions (one Italian and one German) and two airborne divisions were to land on aerodromes. The sea attack was to take place on my Brigade front, most of the air landing on or near by area landing grounds. In this context, my aerodromes were Hal Farr (fighters), Kalafrana (sea-planes), a landing strip at Krendi and the "safe strip" (bombers and fighters) which connected Hal Farr with Luqa. Daniel Beak called a meeting of all officers in two groups outside Valetta and gave a most inspiring talk, warning us of the probability of an invasion in the near future and reminding us how much we owed to our own beloved country. There would be *no* surrenders and *no* prisoners. "Dulce et decorum est pro patria morte." He stressed the importance of physical fitness, exercises and running before breakfast – with his finger pointing at a major who was renowned for his hospitality and good living.

During the first few days of March, raids by JU.88's, escorted by ME.109's, became more intensive: Kesserling obviously feeling his way, and on the evening of March 21st (the date of the March offensive in 1918, in which the Huns nearly reached the Channel ports, which I remembered only too well), standing on the roof of our Mess, we watched wave after wave of enemy planes attacking Ta Kali aerodrome which was north-west of my area. The next day Paul and I went to Ta Kali aerodrome to see the damage done. As we approached the air warning sounded and shortly after squadron after squadron of JU.88's came over, destroying more of our aircraft and the landing strips were pitted with craters. One or two of the bombs fell perilously close to us and for the first time, I think, they were dropping some land-mines, causing enormous craters and blast effects. According to my diary, Paul and I, flat on our tummies, were terrified but fascinated at finding ourselves alive but interested spectators on the target of a large bombing raid.

Shortly afterwards the remnants of a convoy from Alexandria were approaching Malta: Paul and I went to the East Cliff. Two merchant-men had reached the Grand Harbour and apparently the S.S. *Breconshire* had been badly damaged; she was a very fast ship that had run the gauntlet many times with vital cargoes. Being the Sabbath day, the Maltese refused to unload the two ships in the harbour but the Cheshire Regiment gallantly managed to unload some of the precious cargo. Turning to the *Breconshire*, she was still afloat and one of the bombers, flying at roof-top height, fired its rear machine-guns at Paul and me.

Then another tragedy: approaching from the east were several squadrons of JU.88's and Stukas (dive bombers) and we watched Hal Farr, probably the most modern aerodrome in Europe, and the base of four R.A.F. and Fleet Air Arm squadrons, completely destroyed.

His Excellency the Governor, General Dobie, was a very devout Christian and was held in high esteem by the Maltese. His H.Q. was in one of the Knights of St. John's palaces overlooking the Grand Harbour. When the Bosche were raiding the harbour, with his trembling A.D.C. and his Bible, he would ascend to a veranda and watch the raids. The palace was hit earlier in the siege but survived despite the destruction all around. His residence, St. Anton, was some distance from Valetta. Every Sunday he invited one of us Brigadiers to

A typical elderly Maltese peasant like my old goat-herd friend who disliked Mussolini.

lunch and gave us a bag of oranges from his grove. On one such occasion the tragic news of the surrender of Singapore had just arrived. He had been G.O.C. Singapore before handing over to General Percival, and had been responsible for the siting of the guns and, indeed, the whole defence plan of Singapore, expecting that a Japanese invasion would be by sea, whereas the Japs swept through Malaya and over the causeway, attacking the defences from the rear. With his Bible in hand, he asked me to walk with him in his orange grove. He was obviously very, very upset. My reason for this brief reference to this good and gracious man was to opine that he was not the inspiring leader that this beleagured island urgently needed at this critical time. Shortly afterwards, General Lord Gort, V.C., arriving at Kalafrana in the middle of an air-raid, was sworn in as Governor General.

On my early morning walk I usually met an old Maltese with a large flock of goats, which were a staple diet in Malta. On meeting, he would point up to the sky with one hand whilst simulating cutting his throat with the other and saying "Mussolini," and I would do the same. For some reason the Maltese despised the Italians and if Italian survivors were parachuted from their planes one often had to send out two or three men to save their lives.

The bombing was increasing in intensity every day and on one of my early morning walks, with a feeling of sadness, noted that, probably for the first time since Nelson, the Royal Navy had quitted Malta – not a ship to be seen in the Grand Harbour except H.M.S. *Penelope. Penelope*, which was *"The Ship"* in H. S. Forester's novel, had been seriously damaged at the recent battle of Taranto where the Navy sank several Italian ships. She was now bound up against a quay and became known as the "Pepperbox" because of the scores of bomb splinter holes in her hull, but her A.A. guns always joined in the A.A. harbour barrage. What caused us most alarm was the dwindling numbers of our Hurricane fighters which were no match in speed or gunfire for the combined weight of the J.U.88's and ME.109 fighters. It was tragic, seeing so many of our young pilots being shot down. The first Hurricane fighter had not been able to reach Malta and was forced into the sea and, I believe, the pilot drowned. Only Spitfires could save Malta – as they had saved England – and you can imagine our joy when two squadrons arrived and parked on the aerodromes, out of fuel, no ammunition and no personal kit on board, so that they could make the distance. The wily Hun had watched their arrival and came over in hundreds and destroyed most of our precious Spitfires on the ground.

I certainly, pessimistically, felt that Daniel Beak's order to fight to the end, short of a miracle, was soon to materialise. And that miracle was about to happen! Someone in high authority had a miraculous brainwave which, briefly, was as follows. The United Kingdom was to be asked to send more Spitfires. Pens – of stones collected from the shattered surrounding villages – were to be speedily erected on the aerodromes. All available suitable transport carriers, etc. were to be given the tasks of towing each Spitfire into its pen, refuelling it and replenishing ammunition. As a decoy, a minelaying cruiser (the fastest ship in the Navy), loaded with vital medical stores and ammunition, was to come at full speed into the Grand Harbour. All the mobile A.A. batteries were moved into positions around the harbour – and it all worked according to plan!

The Malta A.A. barrage which in conjunction with the Spitfires saved Malta from invasion.

This historic day was 10th May 1941. I went to a mound overlooking the harbour. Having seen H.M.S. *Welshman* arrive, waves of JU.88's, Stukas and ME.109's left Sicily and, to their intense surprise, were confronted by 60 Spitfires. A tremendous air battle was taking place but the bulk of the bombers attacked the harbour where the unexpected strength of the A.A. defence and smokescreen made their bombing erratic. The Stukas were particularly gallant, diving down into the inferno, but unhappily, one or two Spitfire boys were also destroyed. But only one very large bomb fell near *Welshman*, killing one or two ratings and my greatest friend in Malta was wounded but *Welshman* was scarcely damaged.

The air fight continued for a little while. The estimates of the Luftwaffe casualties were considerable but I would say some 40 bombers and several ME.109's were shot down and many others so badly damaged that they may not have reached their bases. Obviously, Hitler's plan to capture Malta by force had failed and, indeed, became an impossibility without air superiority – and so he turned to his second plan, namely, to starve Malta into submission.

Part III – Starvation

Air raids continued, sometimes in strength, and particularly at night, when the enemy frequently dropped anti-personnel bombs which exploded in the air and scattered dozens of small disc shapes which exploded on impact and caused many casualties. But the sufferings of the Maltese had become the priority problem. On 18th April 1942, H.M. King George VI had graciously awarded the island the George Cross – an unprecedented honour for a community and a tremendous boost to morale. Malta was a grossly over-populated island, slightly smaller than the Isle of Wight, with a population of 270,000.

The bombings, particularly in the east of the island and in the Grand Harbour area, had destroyed many thousands of houses but, fortunately, being made of stone, preserved many lives from the effects of incendiary bombs. Thousands of Maltese were homeless and, pathetically, the majority of them were women, children and old people. Fortunately, from the limestone rock upon which Malta is founded, it had been possible to construct large underground shelters and there were also natural caverns. The Islanders flocked into these, not merely for protection from bombs, but for habitation.

The shortage of all necessities of life, e.g. wheat, flour, meat, milk, sugar, vegetables and even fresh water, were getting desperately short, and were severely rationed. Victory kitchens were established where rations were distributed and even goats had to be slaughtered, and most serious was the increasing shortage of kerosene and oil, without

(Imperial War Museum)

People sheltering during an air raid. It was due to the formidable strength of these rock structures that the death toll in the blitzed cities of Malta was not very much higher.

Bombed-out families in Valletta with the remains of their belongings.

(The Times)

which there could be no cooking, lighting or heating. Ordinary necessities such as clothing, shoes, alcohol, tobacco, etc. were out of the question and were unobtainable, except on the "blackmarket" at fantastic prices – and I regret my own Mess was very guilty. When I took over we had seven Rhode Island Red hens, which produced seven eggs a day, one for each of us. But as food shortages gradually increased so, inversely, the egg production from our hens diminished daily, and we all were very hungry until only one egg was produced – and that, I insisted, should be consumed by my youngest and hungriest officer, who, I'm afraid, as Messing Officer, sold the skeletons of our seven old hens for 28 shillings apiece!

London was regularly informed of our estimated survival dates and the latest and final date was August, after which the Union Jack would no longer fly over Malta after 140 years. Two strongly escorted convoys, one from Gibraltar and another from Alexandria failed, with heavy losses. Only two ships reached the Grand Harbour and were unloaded by soldiers in record time. If not a miracle, only a super-convoy with an enormous naval escort could save the George Cross Island. Appreciating this and despite his other tremendous war commitments, Winston Churchill was determined to make this supreme effort which is fully depicted in *"The Malta Convoy,"* by two young officers, one R.N. and the other R.A.F., who took part in this episode. I, of course, in Valetta, was at the receiving end, praying that the convoy would get through.

During June and July the convoy was in the process of being assembled in Scotland, including fourteen merchantmen, all capable of 16 knots which was to be the convoy's speed. The difficulty was that no British tankers were capable of that speed so America graciously sent us the most modern tanker in the world, S.S. *Ohio* (14,000 tons). This vessel was to carry the vital cargo of fuel, oil and kerosene. A British crew took over from the Americans and her captain was Captain Mason. All these vessels had to be equipped with A.A. guns, mostly manned by British soldiers. The Naval escort consisted of two battleships, four aircraft carriers, twelve cruisers and forty destroyers. The armada set forth early in August, rehearsing their convoy drill on the way, entering the Straits of Gibraltar about 6th August. It so happened that agents in Spain gave the Axis constant reports on the convoy's progress and so its naval and air forces were prepared to attack the convoy relentlessly throughout its attempt to reach Malta. From 10th to 14th August the convoy was attacked by JU.88's, Stukas, torpedo bombers, submarines and E-boats (small, speedy and heavily armed launches which were very effective). The Italian navy, not having recovered from Taranto, started off but due to differences between Kesserling and the Italians, and other reasons, thank heavens, they retired.

The most hazardous stretch, the Narrows between Sardinia, Sicily and Malta, had been reached and during the course of the next two or three days there took place probably the most dramatic and horrific battle in our naval history and never had been displayed such an example of endurance and gallantry as that shown by the crews of both warship and merchant seamen. The battleships, being too vulnerable, were sent back to Gibraltar. Two aircraft carriers, two or three cruisers and several destroyers were sunk and of the fourteen merchantmen only five were afloat, including *Ohio,* which, as was to be expected, was the Axis chief target. She had been hit several times and many near misses. A huge gap on her port side, steering and navigating apparatus out of action, engine-room flooded, a broken back and her decks awash, it was extremely doubtful if she would reach Valetta.

S.S. "Ohio" whose arrival in Valetta with vital stores, her decks awash and kept afloat by two destroyers, saved Malta from surrendering.

After stupendous efforts to keep her afloat and moving eventually with a destroyer bound to her on each side and another destroyer towing, she reached the Grand Harbour. The other four survivors, all badly battered, particularly *Brisbane Star,* had reached port the evening before, but the question on the lips and minds of us all was whether the *Ohio* would make it. When she eventually entered the Grand Harbour, a British band played *"Rule Britannia"* on Elma Point and the ramparts were crowded with thousands of people. Captain Mason, after four sleepless days and nights, stood at the salute on his battered bridge, with the remains of a Hun aircraft on the foredeck, the ship was brought to the quay. It was all very emotional, and there were few dry eyes. *Ohio* had saved Malta. Captain Mason was awarded the George Cross and never was that honour more justly awarded. Undoubtedly, Malta's survival halted Rommel's drive to the Middle East – thus contributing to the final outcome of the war. Every year, on 14th August, I telephone Captain Mason who lives in a local village.

Part IV – After the Siege

The bombing continued . . . in fact, one exploded just outside the mess and the corner of my room collapsed and I had to sleep in my office. But the turn of the tide had boosted the morale of the Maltese tremendously and many returned to their villages and began the task of rebuilding their homes. One morning, to my amazement, whom should I meet but my old friend, the goat-man and all his flock, despite the order that all goats were to be slaughtered, and we renewed the procedure of symbolising cutting our throats and saying "Mussolini." I do remember sheltering from a storm in a cave which had obviously been inhabited by goats. I found myself covered in fleas!

About this time Fortress H.Q. telephoned me to expect and accommodate 30 British prisoners-of-war who were the survivors of an Italian ship which had been torpedoed off Benghazi. It reminded me of the experiences of an Indian Army Colonel who had been captured when Tobruk fell. All officers were paraded and in due course General Rommel arrived. He congratulated them on their gallant defence and sympathised with them for being prisoners but he very deeply regretted that all prisoners were to be handed over to the Italians – and how right he was. Admittedly, the Italians were short of rations themselves and a large number of their prisoners were crammed into the hull of a merchantship without food or sanitation. Some of the casualties were left on deck. Sad to relate, the ship was torpedoed. I sent the few survivors to the military hospital.

I mentioned earlier that two R.A.F. squadrons and two Fleet Air Arm squadrons were located in Hal Farr aerodrome which had been destroyed by the Luftwaffe. The R.A.F. moved to a neighbouring village, but the remnants of the Fleet Air Arm decided to put all hands on deck and erect ramshackle accommodation out of the debris. In these very ancient planes they had to fire their torpedoes at water level and, as far as possible, to get away before the guns fired, but their losses were appalling. However, like the submarines, their toll of Axis ships was considerable. Sometimes, *en passant,* I popped in for a chat. One evening I did so and the surviving Lieut. Commander took me into their ramshackle mess, poured me a whisky, telling me that an Axis convoy was approaching Malta and that we were bound to be bombed. They had only two serviceable aircraft – one Swordfish and one Albatross – and they were not giving up. The drill was as follows: on hearing the Island warning, one replenished one's glass; on hearing their own special warning at the top of the airfield, one rushed out and dropped into a slit trench. Sure enough, within minutes, it all happened according to plan and the bombs came raining down but not near us. Soon afterwards these gallant "few" were replaced by Coastal Command Beauforts – a more powerful and up to date aircraft which carried on the good work.

Part V – 231 Brigade

And now to my Brigade. During the threat of the invasion period, the infantry had played an important – indeed, a vital – part in the Island's survival. They had unloaded ships in record time, filled in craters on the runways, often whilst the raids were still going on, built the stone pens for the Spitfires which saved Malta, rescued crews from burning aircraft – and claimed to have shot down two or three enemy planes. The A.A. gunners did have the satisfaction of having a bang at the enemy but the poor old infantry were at the receiving end.

In March and April 1942, it is recorded that over 2,000 tons of bombs fell on the Brigade area. About 150 officers and O.R.s had been killed or wounded, chiefly from the Hampshires and Devons. The latter were furious on hearing that Exeter had been bombed. During the starvation period their rations were reduced from the normal 3200 calories a day to about 1250. We had all lost a stone or more in weight, but what really disturbed "Thomas Atkins" most was not the bombing but having no cigarettes and, when Symonds Brewery was bombed, no beer!

According to a Biblical statement, "Old men shall dream dreams, young men shall see visions." Being relatively in the latter category, my vision was that the 1st Malta Brigade would invade Sicily, to get our own back on the Huns and the Wops who for two long years had tried to bomb and to starve Malta into submission. I ordered each Battalion to march round the Island – and I was not very popular – but despite the ordeals they had been through, they marched past Lord Gort and myself like guardsmen. I told the C.O.s of my vision and my training programme was based on what I called "Exercise Cecilia" which was an imaginary island, which, not so strange to relate, resembled Sicily, but what really was strange to relate was that the imaginary landing strip in our exercise was where the Brigade actually landed two months later. We got down to realistic training, climbing cliffs, rapid marches, exercises with live ammunition, communication with the Navy and so on. Lord Gort was very interested and watched many of the manoeuvres, which called forth from His Excellency, "Malta possessed the finest troops in the world." But I was very fortunate in having the Wessex Regiments in the same Brigade and able to train as a Brigade which was not possible with the other equally gallant regiments which were scattered about the Island.

Meanwhile, General Beak, V.C., D.S.O., M.C. had been relieved of his command and was replaced by General Scobie. Daniel Beak was an outstandingly brave man, although unpopular, but he was just the leader we needed during the siege but not in the post-siege condition – he was far too interfering. He was posted to the 8th Army where his career came to a sticky end.

Meeting Daniel Beak in Newbury after the war I asked him why Lord Gort had sacked him. He said that one of the reasons was because Lord Gort proposed that, when the capitulation of Malta looked a certainty, he wanted to send certain senior officers to Cairo before the white flag went up, as their survival would contribute more to the war effort. Nevertheless, I think that Daniel Beak was right: a commander should stay with his troops to the bitter end.

1st Dorset Regiment marching past at the end of their round the Island 20 mile march.
I felt very proud of them.

General Scobie was a very different personality from his pre-
decessor. Latterly, I had a communications exercise and H.M.S. *Orion*
was most co-operative. General Scobie also suggested that if we
Brigadiers had a Naval friend we might like a day or two aboard.
I had such a friend, Captain Eric Bush, H.M.S. *Euraylus,* who was
about to escort the first convoy to Alexandria for over a year. I went
aboard to the Captain's cabin. It was a very large convoy and, when off
Benghazi the Engineer Commander took me round the ship to the
wardroom for tea. Suddenly, the engines started to accelerate and she
heaved over to the port side. The alarm bell sounded and the
commander said, "Get out quickly, before the doors close." I went up
to the bridge where Eric told me that an Italian submarine had fired
three torpedoes and that he could have pushed the nearest off with a
broom! With the wardroom in the stern, had the torpedo been two
yards nearer, I should not be writing this story. Recounting this
episode at a party to a Royal Marine Major who lives locally, he told
me that he was the officer on watch who saw the torpedoes coming and
gave the warning.

Returning to Malta, General Scobie told me that the Brigade was to
go to Alexandria and was earmarked as an independent Brigade to
invade Sicily – my vision had come true! We had an impromptu party
at the Union Club. Three large transports came into the Grand
Harbour and, with a small escort, set off for Alexandria. It was a sad
day for many. Several of the men had Maltese sweethearts or wives,
and the band of the Royal West Kents played the Regimental marches
of the three battalions as they passed St. Elma Point where the Grand
Knights had defeated the Saracens and the 1st Malta Brigade had
likewise played its part in saving Malta as the Knights had done
centuries ago. I decided not to sail with the convoy but to fly to
Alexandria and to arrange for the reception of the Brigade, such as
entertainments and, particularly, meals after months on a starvation
diet.

The next day, having said farewell to Lord Gort and other Malta
friends, I was flown to Alexandria and stayed with Admiral Leatham
who had been the R.N. commander in Malta. I met the Brigade on the
quayside and they marched to their camp. General Wilson, the G.O.C.
Middle East, inspected the Brigade and was astonished to see such
troops at this stage of the war. Some, particularly in the Hampshires,

had North-West Frontier or Palestine campaign medals. The General was much amused when, in Alexandria, he saw an old soldier tucking into boiled eggs and asked how many he had. "Twenty-one, sir," said the soldier.

We were now to become 231 Brigade and I insisted that our badge was to be a white Maltese cross on a pink background and also to be worn by the supporting units necessary for an independent and self-supporting Brigade group. Malta had been saved.

Why was it necessary when Europe was in German hands, to invade Sicily? The Russians on the Eastern Front and confronted with the military might of the German war machine, were imploring the Allies to invade in Europe, thus relieving the pressure. This, of course, was the ultimate solution, but to breach the Atlantic Wall and advance to the Rhine would take at least a year's special training, organisation and planning. So it was decided to strike at the "soft underbelly" of Europe with American, Canadian and British forces, including 231 (Malta) Brigade, thus eliminating the Italians and diverting German divisions from the Western front.

After a short rest the Brigade was sent to do "Dryshod" training, i.e. to learn the elements of embarking and disembarking on dry land, then to the Suez Canal training camp.

I was then ordered to take my three Commanding Officers, Bill Valentine of the Devons, Bill Spencer of the Hampshires, and Brooke Ray of the Dorsets, up to the 8th Army for battle experience.

My C.O.s attached themselves to various battalions but I had many commitments to cram into ten days. I reported to Monty's Chief of Staff who told me that the Commander in Chief wished to see me and, in a jeep, I proceeded to Sousse where Monty was receiving the acclamations and garlands from the French citizens on being relieved. I met one of his A.D.C.s and he informed him of my arrival. The A.D.C. returned with a message that I was to report to the 51st Highland Division. I accordingly went to 152 Brigade who were very kind to me. The next day the three C.O.s each took me over the battleground of their recent attack on the Romana Feature. In the evening I watched the massed pipers play the "Lament" round the graves of the Highland lads who had fallen. I then called at the H.Q. of General Horrocks, one of the two Corps Commanders, who was very friendly and extremely interested to hear the story of the siege of Malta.

Next day I went to Monty's H.Q., met an A.D.C. to tell him of my arrival and was told that Monty would meet me at tea, which accordingly happened. All he seemed interested in was the character and efficiency of my three C.O.s, never a word about Malta, the survival of which made the battle of El Alamein possible.

I had three days left and went up to the 4th Indian Division, commanded by General Tuker, which was about to go into the last 8th Army battle. The objective was the Garche Feature, a steep and rugged hill held by the Italians. General Tuker was furious at this futile and ridiculous task – and told Monty so. The latter's motive, I understand, was to cause a diversion whilst the 1st and 8th Armies were to link up at Enfidaville, the final battle of the North African campaign. I joined the 5th Brigade, commanded by an old friend, Donald Bateman, who was to carry out the attack. We moved up the line and Donald established his H.Q. in a cleft by the side of the road. The whole of the Divisional and, possibly, Corps artillery bombarded the Feature. The sound of thousands of shells passing over (the music of guns) was like old times in Flanders. The next morning I was on my way up to the front line when I suddenly encountered, about a hundred yards in front, a salvo of small explosions from multi-barrel mortars – a new Hun invention, which I was again to experience in Normandy – and I decided to go no further. The attack was a partial success and possibly achieved Monty's object but the casualties were considerable, including Bill Spencer who was wounded in the right thigh. On the way back I passed an advanced dressing station were casualties were waiting on stretchers. I particularly noted a Gurkha, his right arm in a sling and oozing blood and his head swathed in bandages, but there he lay with a large grin on his face. I asked him about his wounds and he replied that they were negligible but that he had killed three Italians with his Bren gun ". . . pop, pop, pop." I congratulated him but he said that that was of small importance for he had killed three more Italians – then, demonstrating how, by drawing his hand across his throat, i.e. with his kukri. I left him with his smile and hoping that he would survive.

Returning to Cairo I was informed of the strip of coast in Sicily on which I had to land and spent hours working out my plan. By now

231 was a Brigade Group including tanks, artillery, field ambulances and R.E. Field Company and many other sub-units required in combined landing operations.

The Navy, of course, were deeply involved in our planning: all sorts of craft, minesweepers, landing boats, troop ships and naval escorts, etc. Our Naval liaison officers and Naval commander of the operation was Captain Gibson (later Lord Ashbourne), my staff, Willy Tuffil (B.M.), Frank Sadler (S.C.) and Gil Gilchrist (I.O.) and two new staff officers worked from early morning to late at night for many days. I eventually completed my planning and was about to join my Brigade on their training exercises based on the task that lay ahead.

Monty, having finished the North African campaign, came to Cairo and called a meeting of senior officers. Addressing them, he mentioned his Malta Brigade who had been sitting on their bottoms for years in Malta and he was told that they were magnificent troops, which Monty accepted but, mentioning me by name, said that 231 Brigade, in their independent rôle, must be commanded by an officer who had recent experience in battle – in other words, I was sacked. Having gone through the siege of Malta and combining the Devons, Dorsets and Hampshires into a famous fighting Brigade and so looking forward to leading them in Sicily, I was broken hearted. Brigadier Roy Urquhart (latter commander of the Airborne Division at Arnhem on the Rhine) arrived in my office. He was extremely sympathetic and I couldn't have handed over the Brigade to a better warrior for he led it successfully and courageously throughout the campaign in Sicily and Southern Italy.

Extract from *"Malta Strikes Back"* by Major R. T. Gilchrist: "On 19th May, and at a time when planning had reached a positive and constructive stage, it was announced that Brigadier K. P. Smith, O.B.E., was to leave the Brigade to take up an appointment in England, and that his place was to be taken by Brigadier R. E. Urquhart. In normal times such an event would have shaken the Brigade to its very foundations, but now we had no time to trouble about it. We had undertaken a huge work and that work had to go on. It was only afterwards that we realized how much the Brigade was indebted to Brigadier Smith, O.B.E. for everything he had done during his period of command. His particular genius lay in the toning up and training of fighting men. He had taken over the Brigade in the easy-going days at the end of 1941. Quick to realize the quality of the men under his command, he had ruthlessly started to cut away anything which did not come up to the high standard which he demanded. It was a hard time for most of us, but it was not long before we began to realize Brigadier Smith's conception of what a fighting brigade should be like, and to take pride in it. It was Brigadier Smith who brought the Brigade up to such a standard of training, smartness and general efficiency that called forth the remark from Lord Gort, V.C., that "Malta possessed the finest troops in the world." Though at times a hard man to work for, no one could deny the deep love which he held for his Brigade. He took our troubles on himself and fought our battles against the occasional lack of understanding on the part of higher authority and the more frequent stupidity of unimaginative officialdom and often to the detriment of himself."

I must say a word for Monty, after Italy and Sicily had suffered many casualties, Monty assembled the Brigade in Sicily and he praised them for their great work. He then said, "Wherever I go, 231 Brigade will come with me," whereupon there was considerable groaning amongst the Brigade because many of them had not been home for years. Monty then paused for a minute ... "I may be going back to England" – whereupon there were tremendous cheers.

I met Lord Gort in Cairo who told me that everybody was extremely angry and that he could find me another Brigade in the Middle East but possibly I should find myself under Monty again: so he was sending me home with the highest testimonials. I arrived home and went straight to the War Office and was told that I was posted to the 3rd Division which was training in Scotland for the invasion of Europe. I could not have been given a higher Brigade appointment but being in Monty's old Division and the Warwicks in my Brigade, it seemed like "leaving the frying pan into the fire" – but I just had to forget all that and get on with my new job.

Incidentally, 231 Brigade not only landed in Sicily and Southern Italy but also captured Arromanche in Normandy, the only Brigade that had ever carried out three opposed landings.

D - Day, 1944

Part I – Scotland

The 3rd Division, known as the Iron Division, with a great record of service in both World War I and World War II, had covered the evacuation at Dunkirk. Its badge, a small red triangle within a larger black one, and soldiers were proud to wear it! Such was its renown that it had been selected to lead the British Army in the invasion of Normandy!

I duly reported to the Divisional H.Q. at Dumfries and met General Ramsden, a grand old warrior who had commanded a division in the desert and was sent home by Monty when he took over the 8th Army. I then proceeded to my new Brigade – 185 Brigade and met my staff, including Woodrow Wyatt, later a Labour Party Minister.

My three battalions were 1st Norfolks, 2nd Warwicks and 2nd Kings Shropshire Light Infantry. The battalions were located in three villages on the Scottish side of the Border. I met the three C.O.s and had a look at the soldiers, most of whom were very young but who had fought at Dunkirk. We were, for the next twelve months, to undergo the toughest training that the British Army had ever experienced, based of course on the formidable task which lay ahead. That task was to cross the Channel and smash through the Atlantic wall the Germans were constructing from Calais to the Atlantic. Naturally, I eventually saw only the defences facing the 3rd Division, consisting of a wall with 88 m.m. anti-tank guns, mortars and machine-gun strongly fortified emplacements enfilading the beach and with heavily mined and wired obstructions under the water approaching the beach and a minefield and other fortifications inland. The breaching of the wall was merely the first stage, to be followed up by a rapid advance on Caen, about 9 miles inland.

To give a detailed account of the 3rd Division training programme would be superfluous and boring. But, briefly, each battalion had its own training programme. Each one of them had to undergo a fortnight's training at the Divisional Battle School at Moffat, ending up with a realistic attack, closely following an artillery barrage firing live shells, getting through wire and exploding phosphorous mines. Seeing a wretched soldier of the Warwicks, whose clothes were burning, I dashed to him and smothered the smouldering clothes with my hands, during which my right hand was slightly burned. The soldier was hurried off to hospital. On my way back, I called in to see him and his burns were not serious and my hand was cleaned and bandaged. Each battalion had to go to Inverary to practice embarking, disembarking and other landing exercises. Then there was another battle training course on an island near Arran, also a beach landing in Argyllshire. The house and property belonged to a member of the House of Lords and his agent generously allowed the Intelligence section of each battalion to shoot one stag. Then a most important exercise: in turn they were all sent down to tank training areas in Norfolk for combined training with tanks. We three Brigadiers attended a multi-rocket demonstration in which a large type of armoured barge carried a multi-battery of rockets, controlled by a single press-button to fire simultaneously. Then we went to the Tank Corps Depot at Bovington where each of us were put in the driver's seat of a Churchill tank for a day. It was great fun and I challenged Jim Cunningham to a race which he won when I stalled my engine going up a dune.

The Brigade then moved to south-west Scotland and my H.Q. was established at a very large and dilapidated castle near the Solway Firth. One or two minor units were stationed there and my H.Q. was crammed into very inadequate accommodation. I telephoned Divisional H.Q. and was told to move to a suitable house near Dumfries. Outside this castle was a high and steep mound with a small chapel on top. Enquiring about the history of the castle, I was told that it was built centuries ago by a Lowland Chieftain. Periodically, the clansmen would cross the Solway Firth and invade villages in Cumberland, returning with their boats loaded with loot. On one such occasion, coming back with their boats fully loaded, including women and cattle, a sudden storm blew up and their heavily laden craft threatened to sink unless they jettisoned some of their cargo. Should it be the women or the cattle? They decided it should be the women. On getting back to the castle they were full of remorse and built the chapel on the mound. But a curse was cast on the castle that any child born there would die at birth. Now it so happened that the wives of my three youngest officers were very pregnant and likely to deliver their babies in the near future. I told them of the tragic story but allayed their fears by telling them that we were to move the next day.

We had our final Divisional conference at Aberlour on the Spey which brought together our complete invasion play. Our last move, in January 1944, was to Inverness to carry out our first full scale Brigade exercise. The landing took place on the south bank of the Murray Firth. It was bitterly cold and the water was frozen some 50 yards from the shore, through which the troops had to break their way. I managed to get my battle wagon in the first echelon ashore and having done my 50 yards wade I reached my car and changed my wet trousers and pants – for being some 20 years older than the Brigade average, I thought it wise to do so. The troops had to advance two or three miles and take up a position on some higher ground. Tom Rennie and I visited them, mostly sitting in the frozen ground. It was quite impossible to dig shelters or slit trenches and I expected that most of them would catch severe colds or even pneumonia. My Brigade Major, Pay Dayley and I spent the night in the car. The next morning the trucks arrived and took the Brigade to scattered villages near Aberdeen and in which they were billetted in schools, halls, etc. My H.Q. was in a large, empty mansion and my signals section quickly established communication with the battalions and on asking them for their sick parade figures, to my astonishment, they all reported nil return. The only casualty in the whole Brigade of 3,000 men was their Commander who, despite changing his wet clothes and sleeping in a car, developed a dreadful cold, sneezing and coughing!

Whilst here, Divisional H.Q. telephoned me that General Sir Bernard Montgomery would visit the Brigade on the next day. It was still bitterly cold and I ordered the Brigade to parade on a flat, open space and to wear greatcoats. I somewhere found my old Sandhurst greatcoat which I had rarely worn since 1916. The Brigade paraded and awaited the arrival of our Commander in Chief, whose renown was worldwide. After waiting half an hour or so I told the troops to fall out and keep warm. At last, seeing two jeeps approaching, I blew my

General Sir Bernard Montgomery inspecting 2nd K.S.L.I. in Scotland.
From left to right, Lt. Col. Maurice, Maj. Gen. Rennie and the author.

whistle and the Brigade quickly reformed. Monty arrived with Tom
Rennie, took off his coat, showing his rows of medal ribands and
wearing his famous black beret. I called the Brigade to attention, met
Monty, telling him that 185 Brigade was ready for inspection.
Knowing me of old one might have expected him to apologise for
being late or to have greeted me in a friendly way – but not a bit of it. He
told me to order the troops to turn inwards and stand at ease.
Accompanied by General Rennie, a staff officer and myself, he
walked between the battalion ranks, looking at the troops without
saying a word even to the Warwicks, his old Regiment. Arriving at the
Kings Shropshire Light Infantry he was met by the C.O. Jack Maurice,
who always seemed very nervous when he met a senior "Brasshat,"
although as I discovered in Normandy, he was one of the bravest of the
brave. He asked Tom Rennie his opinion of Jack and Rennie told him
that I had a good opinion of him but that he had his doubts. At the end
of the inspection I asked him to address the Brigade. "Of course I will,"
said Monty, "but leave it to me," and he went to the microphone and
told the troops that he had had a look at them and he was delighted to

see that 185 Brigade was living up to the high standard of his old 3rd Division. "Now," said Monty, "come and have a look at me!" and the 3,000 troops rushed up and sat in a half circle. He then gave them a very inspiring talk about what lay ahead and of his confidence in his old Division.

Whilst in the locality I decided to have a look at Aberdeen and, strange to relate, it seemed to resemble the lay-out of Caen, of which I had a map and also was the only person in the Brigade to know our objective. I held a T.E.W.T. (a tactical exercise without troops) attended by all C.O. and Company Commanders.

The time had arrived for us to move south to the Brighton area. The weather was sunny and warm. Going round the troops I would say, "Isn't it lovely to be back in England?" But to my surprise many of them said that they missed the friendliness and hospitality of the Highlands who had invited the soldiers to have a cup of tea and cakes, etc. whereas down here in Kent the inhabitants were totally indifferent in that there had been soldiers, both Canadian and British, in the area, ever since the war began.

I then received a message that His Majesty King George VI would be visiting the Brigade. I selected a parade ground on an estate in which the Warwicks were encamped – and rang up Fortnum and Masons, requesting them to send by express a first-class tea for a "very important personage." The Brigade paraded and I told the C.O. of the Norfolks to arrange that soldiers who had lived on the Sandringham estate to be together in the front rank. His Majesty arrived, nearly half an hour late, and he was extremely apologetic and, pointing his finger at the "Brasshats," said they were to blame. He inspected the parade and then I introduced him to 19 C.O.s, 2 I.C.s and staff officers – and I was breathless at the end, but His Majesty was most impressed and asked Tom Rennie how many mistakes I had made? Then on to a marquee where a sumptuous tea was laid out – sandwiches, cakes, meringues, etc. and I asked His Majesty what he would like to start with, whereupon he said that he never ate at teatime but would love a cup of tea. After he had departed my staff and officers of the Warwicks, who were camped in the park, had a tremendous tuck in!

Time was getting short and all ranks were recalled from leave into a heavily wired encampment which no one was allowed to leave. I then, unexpectedly, received notice from H.Q. that the Commander in

Chief of the whole expeditionary force, General Eisenhower, would visit the Brigade in the grounds of a large country house in Surrey. A beach landing battalion was stationed there and I telephoned them to lay on a cup of tea in the Mess which was a Nissen hut. Lorries arrived and transported the Brigade to the parade ground where they formed a hollow square, as in Monty's inspection and H.M. The King's visit. General Eisenhower arrived about an hour late and apologised profusely – blaming British Railways. I asked him to inspect the parade and he said he would be delighted and stopped to talk with many of them: for instance, seeing a very small man he said he musn't dig in too deep, otherwise he wouldn't be able to shoot – a very tall man was advised he would "have to dig down pretty deep." When the General came to a man wearing a military decoration he would ask him for details of where he won it. It was all in good humour and the troops loved it. I then asked him to say a few words to the parade. Speaking into the microphone, he said how privileged and delighted he had been to inspect this magnificent Brigade of Monty's old Division and how he knew he could count on them in the days to come. How different it had been during Monty's visit in Scotland. The Brigade was transported back to camp and I took the General into the Nissen hut and asked him if he would like a cup of tea. He looked at his watch, which showed 6 o'clock and he said, "It's a bit late for a cup of tea, isn't it?" I mentioned the word "whisky" and he guessed it would be a splendid idea, whereupon a Guards officer, who was attached to the General's staff, quietly asked me not to delay him as we were holding up the railway, and the General heard and said, "What's Bob bellyaching about?" I asked him to have a refill – which he did, despite Bob!

On leaving the hut he told Bob "to send these guys a box of cigars" – unfortunately, it was not our Mess! I accompanied him to his car and he said that he knew I was a busy man but if I would accompany him to the station, some miles away, he would be very pleased. So I popped in beside him and he told me about the American landing beaches and saying what splendid chaps his two senior Generals, Bob Patton and Omar Bradley were. On arrival at the station he invited me into his carriage, which was the Royal Coach, with two guardsmen waiters in short white jackets, and poured me a whisky and we drank each other's health. As I descended to the platform he whispered to me, "I'll see you on Monday." In other words he told me the date of D-Day which no one except the very highest "High ups" knew.

I have expatiated at some length on my own impression of these great soldiers. Monty was undoubtedly an outstanding leader and this was exemplified by his record in the Desert, Sicily, Italy and Normandy. He had the great advantage of mass appeal to his troops, as Wellington had. He was intensely ambitious and unscrupulous but extremely loyal to his 8th Army. On returning to England he had a long list of senior officers, undoubtedly including myself, he was going to sack and replace by his favourite 8th Army Commanders (known as "Monty's boys"). But with one or two exceptions, Winston Churchill, with a stroke of his pen, cut off the rest, one of the exceptions being General Ramsden. Dwight Eisenhower was a completely different character; perhaps not as expert a strategist or tactician as Monty, but just as good a leader. After all, he did two terms of office as President of the United States.

Now, knowing the date of D-Day, I suggested that the three battalions had a completely voluntary and short Church service. I read the lesson at the very well attended Kings Shropshire Light Infantry service and the troops, being conscious that in the very near future some of them might not be in the land of the living, joined in the prayers and sang "Oh God, our help in ages past" with great gusto.

Part II – D-Day, 6th June 1944

Our port of embarkation was Newhaven and my H.Q. ship was a frigate, H.M.S. *Dacres*. On the afternoon of 4th June, the battalion embarked in three transports. I visited them and they all seemed in very good heart. Shortly afterwards I received an order to disembark as D-Day had been postponed until the 6th, so the troops had to disembark and to re-embark the next day. Apparently it was much too rough for landing. I remember that on my way to the harbour I decided to have a long overdue haircut and eventually found a barber who quickly performed the operation. Arriving and boarding H.M.S. *Dacres* I found the Captain, Commander Gotto, R.N. rather anxious, for my haircut had delayed the convoy's departure by a few minutes.

On a sea voyage later I heard a chap talking about a Brigadier who delayed the invasion to get his hair cut! 185 Brigade was the most easterly seaborne formation on the whole invasion front. Our convoy, consisting of H.M.S. *Dacres,* two destroyers, three transports and a few miscellaneous vessels, was part of an armada of over 6,000 ships and landing craft. We sailed out of Newhaven and turned westwards to join up with the invasion convoys which were to proceed through ten mineswept channels. In the evening the sun was setting as we approached Spithead, and one was confronted with a view never to be forgotten. As far as the eye could see every form of warship, battleship, cruiser, minesweeper, landing craft and other types of craft stretched away to the horizon. At a given hour this colossal armada turned towards Normandy. In the Captain's cabin I had one last talk with my staff, went to bed and slept soundly until the fire of hundreds of guns awakened me.

The Divisional plan was roughly as follows: Brigadier (Copper) Cass, commanding 8th Brigade, a tough Yorkshireman who had already fought with distinction in North Africa, was to break through the beach defences and establish a beach-head, including two redoubts, Hillman and Morris, about a mile inland. I was to follow up at maximum speed to Caen, which Monty desperately wanted to capture on D-Day. Jim Cunningham, commanding 9th Brigade, was in reserve and to move up on my right flank between 3rd Division and 3rd Canadian Division. The 6th Airborne Division, commanded by General Gale, was to land during the night and to capture Pegasus bridge which crossed the Orne river and canal which ran parallel to 3rd Division's advance to Caen.

At the final conference at Aberlour in Scotland we were given to understand that having breached one beach defence the only opposition was likely to come from the German 716 Division which was very second-rate. "Speed" was to be the essence of success and the K.S.L.I. were to mount the Staffordshire Yeomanry Sherman tanks, and one company of the Warwicks and of the Norfolks, on bicycles, to move forward on the flanks to pass through Caen and establish fortified road blocks on the other side of the ancient city. For some days previously all sorts of cleverly conceived feints were carried out by all three services to make the Germans believe that the invasion would be in the Pas de Calais. Our complete supremacy in the air prevented German reconnaissance. This was undoubtedly the reason why only one Panzer Division, Rommel's famous 21st Panzer Division, was in our invasion area and even that was 30 – 40 miles south of Caen.

In my Brigade group were three battalions, 7th Field Regiment R.A., the Staffordshire Yeomanry and its 150 Sherman tanks, a Machine-gun Company of the Middlesex, a Field Ambulance and Field Company R.E.

Part III – The Invasion

The immense amphibious operation was on a scale without parallel in the history of war. Never before had an assaulting army, guns and tanks, supported the naval and air bombardment, before they landed. I believe that 7th Field Regiment R.A. fired 200 rounds per gun from their landing craft. All vehicles had to be waterproof – a vital precaution which proved its worth on D-Day. All corps, R.E.M.E., R.A.O.C. and R.A.M.C., had their jobs to do, especially the R.E. Regiment with gapping and obstacle clearing teams who suffered many casualties. The first wave included the tanks of 13/18th Hussars, the South Lancs and East Yorks. The multi-rocket launching craft were a dismal failure, their rockets falling short of the shore and sinking some of our own craft. The first wave ashore met considerable opposition but the South Lancs on the right and East Yorks on the left cleared the beaches on both flanks, but with heavy casualties to both. The next unit to land was Lord Lovat's 1st Commando Brigade whose task was to capture Ouistrehan and to contact Pegasus Bridge and the 1st Royal Marine Commando Brigade, in order to extend to the west, and link up with the Canadians.

1st Commando Brigade were to strike inland and link up with units of 6th British Airborne Division who had captured the Orne canal bridge, now Pegasus Bridge, at Benouville. 8th Brigade's reserve battalion, the Suffolks, to advance and capture two strong German redoubts, code-named Morris and Hillman. All I have written is based entirely on my faltering memory and there are possibly errors in detail. However, my turn had now come to be actively involved with my 185 Brigade, the intermediate Brigade.

On being awakened from my slumber by the sound of the guns, I joined Commander Gotto on the bridge. It was still very rough and I, at last, received the code-word to disembark. I contacted my battalions in code, my last words to their Commanders being "Good hunting."

A landing craft arrived alongside, commanded by a midshipman, with a dead soldier, shot in the previous beach landing, lying in the

185 Brigade landing on Sword Beach.

boat. I got on board and, as we approached the shore defences, the propeller became entangled in the under-water wire and I had to wade ashore, up to my waist in water, while helping a very short officer to keep his head above the waves for a few yards to reach the shore. I made my way through the beach, crowded with armoured vehicles and men and past the beach defences, reaching the Luc sur Mer coast road. I remember seeing a Frenchman getting out of a ruined house and a soldier near me saying, "There's one of the ...." and taking a pot shot at him, but missing! Then a white handkerchief on a stick appeared. How the poor chap had survived the bombardment, heaven knows! Then, standing on the road, Col. Nigel Tapp, the C.O. 7th Field Regiment R.A. and I were suddenly confronted, about 50 yards away, with a wall of flame about 10 feet high and about 150 yards wide. Then, suddenly, it extinguished itself. It was probably a device which the Bosche had not then completed. I never heard of being seen elsewhere.

I established my H.Q. at the gates of Hermanville town hall, and my battalions reported their arrival at their forming up areas. Warwicks on the right, Norfolks on the left and the K.S.L.I. ahead on the Hermanville-Caen road, ready for their advance. The only other unit of my Brigade that so far had got through the beach chaos was the 7th

Field Regiment, R.A., and for a short while was in the front line. Meanwhile I received information that 21st Panzer Division was advancing west of Caen but there were no signs of my Staffordshire Yeomanry having got through the congestion on the beach and remembering the case of a Brigade Commander, one of whose battalions was decimated because he had sent them forward without anti-tank support, I was not going to send either K.S.L.I. or the Warwicks into a tank trap. I accordingly ordered Col. Herdon to move over to the other flank and to advance by the River Orne road.

Lebisey Wood - June 1983

I had decided that, in any case, the Warwicks would be better placed on the left flank. Unfortunately, the Staffordshires were not at full strength, some of their tanks having been diverted to the Hillman battle. Meanwhile, and unknown to me, 9th Brigade was not following up on my right as planned, but had been diverted to Hillman and Pegasus area, and Jim Cunningham himself had been severely wounded. On my left flank the Warwicks were continuing their advance along the Orne road, meeting increasing resistance. Directly I heard that the Yeomanry tanks were getting off the beach I told Jack Maurice to speed ahead and that the tanks would marry up with him. He soon got involved with a heavily wired and fortified strongpoint on the reverse slope of a feature, Perriers sur le Dan. A K.S.L.I. company attacked this formidable obstacle with great gallantry and, despite many casualties, captured it and took many prisoners. Only one and a half tank squadrons had arrived. Why this ghastly chaos on the beach? Obviously the landing had to take place in daylight for control of the bombardment and, indeed, for the assaulting troops and it was expected that at high tide there would be 30 – 40 yards on the beach. But owing to the prevailing winds and exceptionally rough seas, the landing beaches were only 30 – 40 *feet* in depth. Another consideration which was worrying me was that the Suffolks of 8th Brigade had not yet captured the heavily fortified Hillman strongpoint which overlooked the whole of my left flank and had already caused many casualties to the Norfolks advancing on their objective – an important tactical feature which was eventually known as "Norfolk House." The K.S.L.I., continuing their advance on Caen, were eventually caught up by one and a half Squadrons of the Staffordshire Yeomanry tanks, just in time to confront the leading elements of 21st Panzer. With their powerful new 17 pounder anti-tank guns, the Yeomanry quickly knocked out 14 of the German tanks.

The presence of 21st Panzer Division had fully justified my decision to move the Warwicks to my left flank. Meanwhile, a company of the K.S.L.I. had reached Lebisey; two successive company commanders were killed and the company retired to Bieville with a suspicion that they had met 21st Panzer motorised troops. They were within two miles of Caen.

I went over to the left flank in the evening and witnessed a most inspiring and heartening sight. Suddenly, the sky was filled with some 500 aircraft and gliders coming from England to bring to the 6th Airborne Division, who were having a very sticky time, reinforcements, arms and equipment, etc. Some of the gliders came down near where I was standing.

Visiting the well-known war reporter and author, Chester Wilmot at General Crocker's (G.O.C. 1st Corps) request, he told me that on D-Day evening a few 21st Panzer tanks had reached the beaches and the rest were to follow but with the appearance of this enormous air armada, which they interpreted as reinforcements for 3rd Division, they decided to withdraw. Had the Panzer Division reached the beaches it would have been disastrous.

I then decided that the Warwicks should advance on Lebisey early next morning and together with General Rennie went to warn Col. Herdon. The General urged the need for speed. Col. Herdon's starting time was about 8.30 a.m. but unfortunately, his transport carrier and tank guns communication vehicle found they could not cross the marshy ground on each side of a tributary of the Orne and Herdon had to despatch them to a causeway about ½ mile away and, consequently, had to delay his starting time to 9.30, but his two leading companies had already crossed the marsh and he decided that his other two companies should also cross, which they did, up to their knees in slush. Meanwhile, the transport had crossed the causeway and advanced up the Caen road and, tragically, were totally destroyed by German 88 m.m. guns. Some managed to leave the road but were also destroyed. Meanwhile the Warwicks had reached the Lebisey woods and all hell was let loose – Machine-guns, Spandaus, etc. Poor "Jumbo" Herdon was killed instantly, as were many of his troops; his second-in-command, Major Kreyer, gave the order to retire. Col. Herdon was my youngest C.O., an excellent soldier and a great loss. I was very distressed but General Rennie had kept on emphasising the need for speed. But believing that Panzer troops might be at Lebisey in strength, I should have told him that this attack would be courting disaster.

In Bieville, still without further information, I ordered the Norfolks' C.O. to go forward and try to restore the situation – a nebulous commitment. Then I went off myself to get an inkling of the situation but got lost and, finding a barn, rested on a bed of straw until dawn and then returned to my H.Q. at Bieville. My H.Q. was in the ruins of a large chateau which the R.A.F. had destroyed, belonging to the brother of Leon Blum, the former Socialist President of France. It had been the headquarters of the German Commander in Chief of the Normandy coast defences. There were enormous cellars with hundreds of empty champagne bottles. Pat Dayley, my B.M., was naturally wondering what had happened to me but during my absence he had found a full bottle and, returning extremely weary and depressed, the champagne cheered us up considerably. Later on I went to the orchard where the Warwicks were encamped and was very glad to see so many survivors of Lebisey. Fortunately, the high corn had helped to cover their retreat. I don't know what casualties they had suffered but I would approximate about 150 killed, wounded and missing.

For the next three weeks two battalions were in the front line and one in reserve. We were subjected to a good deal of shelling and multi-barrelled mortars. I visited the battalions most days but rarely saw Jack Maurice for he was usually up in the front line, particularly if the shelling and mortaring was heavy. Dear Jack was killed a few days later outside Caen. Despite the disappointment at not reaching Caen the morale of the Brigade was restored and an organised attack on Lebisey was planned but was cancelled at the last minute.

General Rennie had been wounded and his place was taken by General ("Bolo") Whistler, a great soldier and well known to Monty who had visited him and, being bitterly disappointed at my not having reached Caen, suggested that I was on the old side and not up to the stresses which lay ahead. In his report, Bolo confirmed Monty's doubts but said that on D-Day I led my Brigade with great gallantry and should retain my rank as Brigadier. Thus, sad to relate, Lebisey being my Waterloo, as Napoleon was banished to St. Helena, I was, metaphorically, banished to Madagascar, although as a commander and not as a prisoner!

Understandably, I was broken-hearted at leaving my beloved Brigade after a year's arduous training in Scotland and their gallant performance on D-Day, on D + 1, and indeed during the next three weeks when they were constantly mortared and shelled. No Brigade could have done better and they continued to keep up that standard in the Iron Division until the end of the war and beyond.

It finally took three Divisions to capture Caen but I was expected to capture it in one day. Would it ever have been possible to achieve our goal? I was asked that question by an American army officer who has written a book on the Normandy invasions. My answer was in the affirmative providing the following pre-requisites had been met:–

1.   That the 8th Brigade capture Morris and Hillman fairly quickly.
2.   That the supporting armour disembark in time, to fully support the drive on Caen by 185 Brigade.
3.   The 185 Brigade and Staffordshire Yeomanry reach Caen before the 21st Panzer Division arrived on the scene.

4.   That there was no unexpected heavy opposition, particularly around Lebisey.

None of these four provisions materialised and that's why Caen did not fall on D-Day. There were, however, two other common factors, namely that chaos on the beaches caused by the heavy weather and exceptionally high tide and our lack of Intelligence, both as regards enemy movements and dispositions and also the lay out of the country, particularly Lebisey. I later heard the good news that my old Malta Brigade 231, now serving with 50 Division, had captured Arromanche and Bayeux.

Twenty years later. The three Infantry Brigade Commanders, Copper Cass, Jim Cunningham and the author on Sword Beach.

EPISODE 12

Madagascar

At the end of June 1944, I left Normandy and the War Office informed me that I had been appointed Commander of East African Command Sub-Area, including Madagascar, Mauritius and the Seychelles (and a number of smaller islands). I was to report to East African Command H.Q. for further orders. I was delayed in Kenya and did not arrive in Diego Suarez until late September. I was met at the airport by staff officers and French officials, ferried across the harbour to Diego Suarez. Madagascar now belonged to the Free French but in view of the Japanese submarine menace, the defence of the Island was a British responsibility. Actually, a year or two before, a British force had successfully defeated the Vichy French and handed it over to the Free French. There was a graveyard near Diego Suarez in which about 100 British soldiers were buried.

Diego Suarez was a depressing town but its harbour was one of the largest and most attractive in the world. Its one major drawback was a narrow and rocky entry where many ships had foundered. The officers mess, which had been the headquarters of the old French Army, was delightful: a large dining room and anteroom, a long veranda overlooking the harbour and separate rooms for ten officers. On the ground floor was the guard-room and Kings African Rifles sentries and accommodation for the servants, etc. In the harbour were two Catalina and Sunderland flying-boat squadrons, commanded by an old R.A.F. friend, Wing-Commander Carter. Anti-submarine patrols, particularly over the Mozambique channel which was on the mercantile shipping route to South Africa and the Cape, were their main function. At Jaffreville, on higher ground than Diego, a K.A.R. battalion was stationed and also an officers club to which one could escape from Diego for a few hours.

In the south of the island two K.A.R. companies were stationed, commanded by "Tishy" Thornhill, an officer of my regiment. The garrison of Diego consisted of about 200 British troops, mostly Corps troops, R.E.M.E., R.A.O.C., R.A.S.C. and R.A.M.C. – and a hospital and nursing staff. Headquarters of the French Government and Army, including some Senagalese battalions and French officers and N.C.O.s were at Tananarive in the centre of the island and about 2,000 feet higher up than Diego. There were also a few local native units under French command – thus a general picture of the air and land defence forces of Madagascar. There were also a few French and British naval vessels in the harbour. Coming from starving England I found the mess menu both colossal and delicious – fruit, fish, meat and vegetables. For lunch, a large bowl of oysters as big as saucers and carafes of Algerian wine were on the table. Our cook was Chinese, and a very good one too.

My staff were a mixed bunch: an excellent gunner colonel and one or two others but my chief staff asset was Neil McPherson, later Lord Dumalbyn, who spoke French fluently and was my Liaison Officer. The Commander in Chief of all French troops in Madagascar was General le Long – of whom more about later. I had now to start visiting the other islands in my area and my first selection were the Pamanzi Islands in the Mozambique channel. A smaller number of K.A.R. troops formed the garrison together with a few French residents and officials. Strange to relate, the natives lived and thrived on the good old "gobble gobble" turkey and as Yuletide was approaching I took back a brace to Diego.

My next visit was to Mauritius where a K.A.R. detachment was stationed and a number of British manned coastal batteries. I stayed with the Governor, Sir Hugh McKenzie, who lived in an attractive house surrounded by woods in which were wild deer. I visited the coast defence batteries and found the men, who were, understandably, very "browned off." I then inspected the K.A.R. and Mauritius troops and visited a museum where, in a glass case, was the only known specimen of the long extinct dodo. I was interested to see that at least one street and building were named after General Gordon of Khartoum who was stationed there as a Sapper subaltern. The Mauritians were of mixed blood. The island had once belonged to France and there are still many French families. There was a story about a naval battle in which the wives of both the French and British admirals were *très enceinte* and the admirals mutually agreed to cease-fire whilst their respective wives were taken to the same hospital. Both deliveries were successful, the battle recommenced – and the British won! I visited Mauritius two or three times during my tour – anything to get away from Diego.

I was then flown to the Seychelles, a most beautiful group of islands. I stayed with the Governor in his large and ancient house in the gardens of which was a large tomb containing the remains of the last French governor, who surrendered the Seychelles to the British. On the west of the main island, Mahe, a number of retired Indian Army officers had made their homes many years before. There was a Seychelles battalion and two or three coastal batteries were manned by British gunners who, as in Mauritius, had been years away from home and found life very boring.

There was a Seychelles battalion for home defence which I also inspected. Before I arrived, on one or two occasions, I cabled the British Colonel who was O.C. Troops, to fix up some deep sea fishing which he kindly did. Accordingly, we got into a rowing boat and proceeded to the fishing water. I was asked to be the fisherman. One sat with a large coil of very strong fishing line with a three pronged hook baited, I think, with meat, which was dropped into the sea and let the coil gradually unroll, hoping to get a bite. In due course I did. I suddenly felt my line jerking and started to reel in with great difficulty. Obviously, I had caught a very big fish, when suddenly my coil relaxed and I wound up with just the head of a very large fish on the hook. Sad to say, a shark had consumed the rest of the fish. These smooth waters were teeming with fish, including the sail-fish whose fins above water looked just like the black sails of a boy's toy sailing yacht on a pond.

Opposite Mahe was a small but very lovely island with palm trees, coconut trees, ferns and flowers. According to local folk lore it was the original Garden of Eden. There was one enormous coconut tree, the fruit of which was reported to be an aphrodisiac. On the Mahe beaches were unique and very large seashells and I brought some home as ornaments. As usual I could write at length on these beautiful islands.

Now back to Diego Suarez: I'm afraid that these episodes are very much out of sequence. On Christmas Day I visited the hospital, and the small messes of the garrison troops and arrived back at our mess very late for my turkey lunch. At that time of year, besides being hot and sticky, Diego was subjected to a horrible wind, carrying a form of sand which penetrated doors, windows and everything. On such a day Neil McPherson and I started off in a jeep on a very bumpy track to Majunga. We were greeted by the French officers, inspected their batteries and were taken into the mess for an aperitif. They then suggested that Neil and I would like a bathe on a delightful beach – and how we enjoyed that bathe. Returning to the mess for another aperitif and lunch, the French major told us that in honour of our visit we were to have an English lunch – a meal I shall never forget. The menu was hors d'oeuvre, oysters, tomato soup, fish, roast beef, rice pudding, cheese, coffee and, of course, all swilled down with Algerian wine. After bidding our hosts farewell, Neil and I proceeded on our sweltering and bumpy journey back to Diego. My gastronomics being somewhat upset, I went straight to bed and remained there for the next 24 hours.

In Diego every week I held a meeting in my office with the three local senior French authorities: the civilian resident, who was a very nice man, the French Naval Commander and Col. Alegreni, the Military Commander. Alegreni was an odd character of very doubtful racial origin and had a beautiful wife of whom he was exceedingly jealous. Apparently all three disliked one another: at the meeting they jabbered at one another and Neil interpreted. After the meeting all three would telephone me telling me what ghastly fellows the other two were. However, we invited all three to a dance – with Alegreni's watchful eye on his wife and current dancing partner, including myself.

I have not mentioned one of my islands, namely Rodriguez. It was located about 500 miles south-west of Mauritius. It was an extremely important cable station for the deep sea cable across the Indian Ocean to Australia. Two Mauritian coast defence batteries were stationed there and I was told that a form of partridge thrived on the island. The only contact with civilisation was a dirty old tramp steamer that visited the island once a month from Mauritius. It appeared that the island had never been visited by the "Brasshats" of East African Command, although one General and staff did try to reach it, but the Indian Ocean swell made it too dangerous for the flying boat pilot. But I was determined to have a shot at getting there. The French naval captain at

Diego invited me to a party to welcome the British Commodore of the East African fleet and I told the Commodore of my disappointment at not getting to Rodriguez – and to my surprise and delight he simply said, "I'll get you there."

I have mentioned General le Long of Tananarive. Every now and again he popped down to Diego. He always seemed pleased to see me, embracing me with both arms and pecking me on both cheeks, *à la mode Francaise*. He invited me to visit him for two or three days at Tananarive. I was met at the airport by a comely French lady in uniform who said that she was one of the General's A.D.C.s but regretted to say that he was confined to bed with fever and that a French colonel would look after me and take me round and I was to enjoy a very happy visit.

I called to pay my respects to the Governor General and Madame Pierre de Saint Mort and met that charming lady who told me that I would be invited to dinner the next day. She then asked me if I would like to visit the bazaar in the market square, to which she escorted me and I bought a couple of beautifully carved heads of a Malagasman and woman. Madame then asked me if I would like a delectable French dinner. Jokingly, I said, "Yes, but not snails." Whereupon she said, "What about frogs legs?" and I, somewhat sceptically, said that I would be delighted. and sure enough, a bowl of frogs legs was produced at dinner and they were truly delicious!

My friend, the French colonel, took me to the French N.C.O.s mess where I said a few words about the *Entente Cordiale* which they seemed to like and then to a trout farm near the officer's mess. I have never seen such large trout and a French officer told me to point to the one I would like for lunch and, indicating a particularly large one, it was netted. The Colonel said, "Mon Général," (which I was always called in Madagascar as a French Brigadier was "Un Général de Brigade"), come into the mess and you will be eating your fish in half an hour." Lunch was served and I was given a huge, boneless chunk of trout which was delicious. The colonel then took me to see the remains of Queen Ranavelo's palace, particularly the huge dining hall which was a museum piece.

Ranavelo must have been one of the most attractive, brutal, licentious and powerful characters in history. In the middle of the dining hall was a huge tree trunk several feet thick, deeply dug into the ground and providing the central support of the roof. The story was that Queen Ranavelo had seen the tree in the south of the island and ordered it to be cut down and dragged to Tananarive. It took more than a thousand men, hundreds of whom died, to drag it there. On my last evening there was a dance at the officers club and I went to bed early, asking the A.D.C. to awaken me at 5 a.m. but he overslept and we arrived at the aerodrome just as the weekly plane to Diego was taking off. I was very angry, when suddenly a villainous looking oldish man, wearing many war ribands, introduced himself as Captain Roberto, came up, seized my suitcase, telling me that he would take me to Diego Suarez. He bundled me into his ancient "kite" and off we started. Sitting by the side of Roberto, he never stopped talking. Apparently, this old plane was his livelihood and he flew to all parts of Madagascar. Suddenly, he pointed at a small village and a landing strip and, telling me that a lovely woman and her family lived there, we were descending to see her. We landed on the strip and his lady friend and family rushed out to meet him. They embraced, went into her house, had a glass of wine, more embracing and off we went again. Later on, Roberto again pointed down saying that he had a beautiful friend living there and we would pop down and see her, but very loudly and with great determination, I said, "Non, Non, Roberto!" explaining that my staff at Diego would be wondering what had happened to me. However, we arrived very late and found one or two of my staff anxiously awaiting my arrival, and the problem of Roberto's payment was settled. Back in my office with piles of correspondence to deal with, the telephone rang and a lady who was the wife of one of the officers of my Regiment, serving with the K.A.R. in Mauritius, telling me that she had just arrived at Diego harbour in the weekly mail boat from Mauritius and that the Captain had tried to molest her several times and as she had to return by the same ship she was very alarmed. I promptly went down to the quayside, met the captain, who was an unpleasant looking middle-aged man, and told him that if there was any more trouble, I would report him to his company and to the police. On the return journey, he appeared to be very subdued and there was no more trouble, so the lady advised me at a Regimental gathering some years later.

And now for my final and most perilous episode. About lunch-time in the mess, I answered the phone and in a very Scottish voice my caller announced that he was Lieutenant Black and that he was

Captain of H.M.S. *Shapinshay* and that he had been ordered to take me to Rodriguez. I asked him to lunch and boarded H.M.S. *Shapinshay* at about 3 p.m. She was an old North Sea trawler, painted grey with a small gun on the forward deck. She had been a patrol boat off Mombassa and was going to the docks of Mauritius to have her hull scraped. My cabin was very tiny where I dumped my suitcase (together with my shotgun for the partridge!) and off we sailed. It was terribly hot and stupidly I took off my shirt and went to sleep on a deckchair on the Captain's bridge – and woke up looking like a lobster! I had an early evening meal and went to bed; however, my skin had started to peel and blister and I had a sleepless night. At breakfast the Captain told me that he had just heard that a cyclone was approaching from the direction of Mauritius and that we were now steaming southwards to avoid it. The calm sea now started to get rougher and rougher and for two days we battled on. I was very seasick and wishing that I had never heard of Rodriguez. The Captain, regretfully, decided to return to Diego – about 200 miles away. We were sitting in his cabin when a seaman from the engine-room came in and reported a cylinder piston ring had broken which reduced our speed to one knot, just enough to keep our bow into the mountainous waves. The Captain was very upset and confided to me that this was the first time he had ever been to sea – news which, I admit, was not very cheerful and he delved into a cupboard and produced a bottle of "the wine of Scotland," which we both sorely needed. Then another knock at the door and the engine-room chief came in and in a broad Yorkshire accent (all the crew were Yorkshire fishermen) said that exactly the same thing had happened some years ago in the North Sea and that an improvised piston ring was made out of a bucket handle. The Captain told him to get on with it if they had a bucket. Feeling somewhat sceptical, I went to the stern and I remember two enormous sharks swishing backwards and forwards between the waves. Obviously, one was saying to the other, "Look at him, he will make a tasty meal." The bucket handle was successful and H.M.S. *Shapinshay* steamed back to Diego at 7 knots, 1 knot faster than her previous record. A night or two later I went to the Joffreville Club and Lieutenant Black was there and gave me the bucket handle which, sad to relate, I forgot to bring back.

I now come to the end of my comparatively short Madagascar saga. The Hitler war was nearing its end but the Burma campaign was at its height. Moreover, the Free French now wished to take over the island completely. Accordingly, I was ordered to take over command of the 29th East African Brigade in Moshi Tanganyika (Tanzania).

I was naturally very sad not to have continued with 3rd Divison in the Normandy landings on D-Day, but my five months in Madagascar and the other islands was a very happy and exceedingly interesting experience. On leaving I had very kind leters from the Governor in Tananarive and from the General.

The Kings African Rifles

The 29th Brigade comprised Uganda, Kenya, Tanganyika and Nyassa battalions, each a thousand strong. The purpose of the Brigade was to provide and train reinforcements for the 11th East African Division and independent brigade in Burma. I reported to H.Q. at Nairobi and General Hawkins decided to send me to India and Burma to gain knowledge in jungle warfare which would be useful in my Brigade training programme. I went to Delhi to meet the Director of Training, an old friend of mine, to Dera Dhun, the Indian Sandhurst, then on to Burma where I visited some of the 11th East African Division battalion commanders; the Division now being out of the line, and gleaned much useful knowledge. I was flown back to Cairo and up the Nile in a flying boat to the Uganda, Kenya border and then in a Hudson, an aircraft which, remembering a disastrous episode in my Coasal Command days, I always distrusted. My two young pilot officers were late – and had obviously lunched very well. Looking at my diary the date was Friday the 13th. At the end of the runway was a tree! However, we skimmed over it, and arrived safely at Nairobi.

I reported to General Hawkins, who warned me that I had a very delicate and difficult task to perform, namely to inform the Somali Battalion that they were to be disbanded. The Somalis were recruited from a much disputed territory between Kenya and Somaliland. They were devout Muslims, and wore different uniforms to other K.A.R. units whom they regarded as inferior beings. General Smallwood told me that they had refused to cut the grass round their huts, saying that it was "Nigger work" and their few white officers obviously had no control over them. I went straight away to their camp and told the Adjutant to assemble them – about four hundred – and they were told to sit down. I then addressed them, starting off with a lengthy Arabic adoration of Allah and his prophet, Mohammed, which I had learned in Nigeria – and to my pleasant surprise they seemed to appreciate it. No officer had ever addressed them in that way. I then handed over to the Somali Regimental Sergeant Major who spoke English – and I gave forth a packet of "white lies." "Tell them, Sgt. Major, that I have good news for them. As the Japanese war looked like ending (which it didn't, until the atomic bomb was dropped on Hiroshima and Nagasaki), His Majesty the King intended to send home those soldiers who had served him most loyally and who more so than the Somali Regiment!" And they were truly delighted. In actual fact, on one or two occasions in Burma they fought well but generally they were a confounded nuisance. Anyhow, they left peacefully in lorries for their homeland the next day.

Moshi was on the southern edge of Kilimanjaro which was the highest mountain (19,000 feet) in Africa and one of the most picturesque in the world, with its permanent snowcap which, especially at sunset, was beautiful. The thickly wooded slopes were obviously an excellent training ground for jungle warfare. The troops constructed a makeshift village and Japanese *sangar* (strong-points). Every company had to spend a few days intensive training there including some exercises with live ammunition and, of course, night patrols at which the Japanese were particularly experienced. On the plain near the camp were rifle ranges. At Nairobi one of the senior staff officers, a friend of mine, Cuthbert Alport (later Lord Alport), supplied us with our considerable ammunition requirements. The Askari (K.A.R. soldier) liked being drilled on the square and became quite smart. The Moshi area was renowned for its big game. I never saw a lion, elephant or buffalo, but came perilously close to a rhinoceros.

Driving to Nairobi, as I did every month, having to travel 300 miles, I had to start before daylight. My driver and I had literally to beat our way through herds of zebra which were mesmerized by the lights of the car. One day, in the Rift valley, on my way to Nairobi, a large giraffe came out of the bush and lolloped along in front of us. Travelling at 70 m.p.h. I slowed down. In front of the giraffe was a culvert and bridge which, apparently, he did not like the look of, turned round and landed with his tummy on the bonnet of the car and partially through the windscreen. All I could see was giraffe and, thank heaven, I did not crash into the culvert. However, the giraffe scrambled off and lolloped away into the bush, looking none the worse for wear and, miraculously, the bonnet of the strong American car was not even dented. I should be in the *Guinness Book of Records* as the man who carried a giraffe on his car for 20 yards!

On one occasion, staying with friends in their lovely house near Lake Naivasha, I decided to buy 200 acres of luscious pasture with all sorts of game browsing and many hippopotamus in the reeds on the lake, all at £10 an acre. I thought that perhaps my family might like to settle there but they did not wish to do so. When a businessman from Nairobi flew to England and offered me £15 an acre I accepted. He and a Nairobi friend decided to split it and each built a bungalow on his plot. Unhappily, he was later brutally murdered by the Mau Mau.

Now back to Moshi. Formerly it had been the H.Q. of a K.A.R. battalion and before that, I believe, of the Germans. I had an unusually large staff of twelve officers and a chaplain, and an excellent and happy lot of chaps they were. One of them apparently on guest nights used to crunch glass and swallow it – a practice I forbade! One had been a shopwalker in Harrods and he took the Brigade Signallers and heliographed messages from about 12,000 feet up on Mt. Kilimanjaro. My two senior officers were outstanding. Each battalion had about 16 offficers and 30 British W.O.s and N.C.O.s – the latter, as in the Islands Area, were not altogether happy. There was only one hotel in Moshi, "The Lion Cub," and officers were usually its customers, but the N.C.O.s had nowhere to go. My friend Cuthbert Alport allowed me to commandeer a large hut which had probably been a store. There was in Moshi an Italian prisoner-of-war camp, whose internees, being excellent carpenters, transformed the hut into "The Buffalo Arms" in a very short time, complete with furniture, etc. and a well-stocked bar sent from Nairobi. It made all the difference to the contentment of the N.C.O.s. They invited me to their celebration night and insisted that I should sing a song, and I reluctantly sang an old army song:–

> *"Oh, how I hate to get up in the morning,*
> *Oh, how I love to stay in bed,*
> *But the hardest blow of all*
> *Is to hear the bugle call,*
> *'You've got to get up,*
> *You've got to get up when it's morning,*
> *You've got to get up, you've got to get out of bed.'*
> *Some day I'm going to kill that bugler,*

> *Some day you're going to find him dead.*
> *He'll never sound another note,*
> *I'll ram that bugle down his throat –*
> *And then I'll spend the rest of my days in bed."*

When the Brigade was disbanded I received a very gracious letter from them which I still have. Many of the officers, as in the case of the N.C.O.s, had been in East Africa for some years although a few of them had homes in Kenya. I therefore decided to turn the former Brigade Command bungalow into an officers club and I settled in a small bungalow near the mess.

A word about my Askaris: the Ugandan, Kenyan and Tanganyikan were to me, good, keen and well-disciplined but, as a comparative newcomer, more or less the same with the Tanganyikans possibly a little tougher. My favourites were the Nyassa (Malawi) battalion. They were smaller in stature, peasant farmers and tribesmen, untainted by too much contact with civilisation. Their C.O. asked me to inspect them. The whole battalion was on parade and as the C.O. and I approached the whole battalion came to meet us with their rifles in the air and much shouting. For a moment it looked like a mutiny and I was a little perplexed until the C.O. who lived in Nyassaland, explained that it was the Nyassa tribesmen's salute to their chief.

At last V.J. day arrived, and during the following week the 29th K.A.R. Brigade was to be disbanded. Accordingly I ordered a farewell ceremonial parade. One of the battalions had, enterprisingly, formed a band. The Brigade formed up by battalions which I inspected slowly, driving by in a jeep, presenting two or three medals and then returned to the saluting base and the 4,000 officers and men marched past like Guardsmen. I sent a letter to all C.O.s to be read out to their men, thanking them for their services and hoping that they would have happy recollections of their soldiering days. The next day we had a farewell party in the officers club and my four commanding officers presented me with a large cigar box with the badges of all four regiments carved on it. The senior C.O., with a few complimentary and somewhat emotional words, presented it to me.

The lorries came in and, day by day, the battalions were taken to their respective battalion depots for discharge. The last to go was the Nyassa battalion – and very fortunately so, for I received a telephone call from the civil service commissioner telling me that the WaChaga (the tribesmen of the Kilimanjaro slopes) had descended and were

The disbandment parade.

looting the shops of Moshi which, as in all East African countries, were owned by Indians (the "Duka Wallahs") and within a very short time the Nyassans were there and drove the WaChaga looters away. The next day I received my orders for home. As I drove away the Nyassans lined the road on both sides.

In due course I embarked at Mombassa for home. In retrospect I was glad to have commanded the 29th Brigade. With the wonderful training area on the slopes of Kilimanjaro, I was able to create a training formation into a first class fighting brigade. An opportunity which the 11th Division in Burma had never had. "Something attempted, something done was earned a night's repose." I was kindly mentioned in despatches. Arriving in England I went to the War Office but was told that there was no prospect of another appointment and so I decided to retire from the Army.

At that time, of course, all the many Divisions formed during the War were being disbanded and all the Regular, Divisional and Brigade Commanders, including myself, were basically Lieut.-Colonels or Majors and were reduced to their substantive rank. Hence, having been a temporary Brigadier for four and a half years, I decided to retire with the rank of Brigadier for life.

Epilogue

And so I come to the finale – the story of thirty years as an infantry soldier (P.B.I.) during which I was privileged to serve my country, that little island set in a silver sea upon which the sun never set and the centre of the greatest and most benign Empire in history. In both World Wars, our imperial troops of all three services from Canada, Australia, New Zealand, India, South Africa and even our African Colonies, came thousands of miles over oceans and deserts to support their Mother Country in her fight for freedom. In both World Wars our fatal casualties totalled a million and a quarter, and probably more, of whom over two hundred thousand from overseas paid the supreme sacrifice and never returned to their homelands.

Later on ensued that diabolical episode, the Yalta Conference, at which Stalin, Roosevelt and the ailing Winston Churchill agreed to disintegrate the British Empire; a decision which Winston bitterly regretted on his return.

> *"Tis not the Frontier but the failing heart*
> *When the Empires crack, collapse and fall apart."*

There is much sagacity in the following lines but soldiers, like us all, differ. Some actually liked action but most hated it. But in the trenches we did think of sunlit homes and our families.

> *"Soldiers are citizens of Death's grey land*
> *They draw no dividends from time tomorrow,*
> *And in the grave hour of destiny they stand,*
> *Each with his joy and each with his sorrow,*
> *But soldiers warned for action*
> *Seek flaming fatal fortune with their lives,*
> *But soldiers are dreamers and when the guns begin*
> *They dream of sunlit homes, sweethearts and wives."*

And I end on a more joyful note by quoting the ultimate verse of the *Rubaiyat* of that ancient Persian philosopher, Omar Khayam:

> *"And when thyself with shining foot shall pass*
> *Amongst the guest stars scattered on the grass*
> *And in the joyous errand reach the spot where I made one*
> *Turn down an empty glass."*

The Kings African Rifles Brigade, on the march, near Moshi